Choctaw and Chikasaw Indians ..

CHOCTAW AND CHICKASAW INDIANS

77
73

Mr. CLAPP presented the following

HEARINGS BEFORE THE COMMITTEE ON INDIAN AFFAIRS ON THE CHOCTAW AND CHICKASAW INDIANS

January 30, 1907 – Ordered to be printed

COMMITTEE ON INDIAN AFFAIRS,
UNITED STATES SENATE,
Washington D. C., January 23, 1907.

Committee met at 10 o'clock

Present—Senators Clapp (chairman), McCumber, Clark (Wyoming), Long, Warner, Sutherland, Brandegee, Dubois, Clark (Montana), Teller, and Stone

The committee having under consideration the following proposed amendment to the Indian appropriation bill—

That the Secretary of the Interior is hereby authorized and directed to transfer from the Choctaw and Chickasaw freedmen rolls to the rolls of citizens by blood of said nations the name of any person who is of Indian blood or descent on either his or her mother's or father's side, as shown by either the tribal rolls, the records prepared by and in the custody of the Commissioner to the Five Civilized Tribes or the Department of the Interior, or by any governmental records in the possession of any bureau, division, or commission, or any of the departments of the Government, or any of the courts of Indian Territory, and persons having rights conferred by this act shall be entitled to establish only by evidence their descent from persons of Indian blood and recognized members of the tribes as appears from any such record. *Provided further,* That nothing herein shall be construed so as to permit the filing of any original application for the enrollment of any person not heretofore, and at the time of the passage of this act, enrolled as a freedman of either the Choctaw or Chickasaw nations, or who has an undetermined application for such enrollment now pending, it being the purpose of this act to provide only for correction of the enrollment of persons of Choctaw or Chickasaw Indian blood who have been enrolled as freedmen of said nations, and no limitation of time within which to file original applications or to perfect appeals heretofore fixed by law shall be construed as a bar to rights conferred by this act, and any person so transferred may contest any allotment heretofore made to which he or she had a superior right at the time of his or her erroneous enrollment. *Provided, however,* That such contest shall be instituted within ninety days from the date of such transfer, and that patent has not issued for such allotment.

in relation to the application of certain persons of mixed Indian and negro blood, arbitrarily enrolled as freedmen before the Commission to the Five Civilized Tribes, for a transfer of their names from the freedmen roll to the roll of citizens by blood of the Choctaw and Chickasaw nations

Appearances—Webster Ballinger, Albert J. Lee, for petitioners

Mr. BALLINGER. We are attorneys for applicants of mixed Indian and negro blood, who have been enrolled as freedmen and not as citizens, by reason of their Indian blood, birth, and residence in the Choctaw and Chickasaw nations.

By Mr. LONG:

Q. You seek to have them transferred from the freedmen roll to the Indian roll?—A. Yes, sir.

Q. Under section 4, Five Civilized Tribes, you claim that transfer can not be made?—A. Yes, sir.

There are two questions involved in this controversy, viz:

1. Is a child born to a negro mother, either herself at one time held in involuntary servitude, or whose ancestors were once held in involuntary servitude, and whose father was a full-blood Choctaw, or vice versa, barred from receiving property conveyed and secured to him by the treaties with, and laws of, the United States?

2. If a strain of blood descending from an ancestor once held in involuntary servitude does not bar a person from taking real and personal property under the treaties and laws with and of the United States, have such persons been deprived of their legal property rights by officers of the Government charged with the duty of administering the Choctaw and Chickasaw communal estate and by recent indirect and ill-conceived acts of Congress?

By Mr. BRANDEGEE:

Q. You quote the language we put in the bill last year?—A. Yes, sir.

Q. Is there anything in any of the supplementary agreements that modifies the uses of this treaty (1830) as to the descendants of these people?—A. Not a word can be found in any treaty or law that modifies any of them. The treaty of 1830—

Mr. LONG. There are limitations as to time?

A. Yes; there are limitations as to time.

Mr. BALLINGER. The question is, Have they been barred of those rights by the holding of executive officers?

Now, let us look to the treaties and laws with and of the United States to ascertain what rights were conferred upon what people by said treaties and laws.

TREATY OF 1830.

Article II of the treaty of 1830 conveyed a tract of land situated west of the Mississippi River, and which is the identical land now being allotted in severalty to the members of the Choctaw and Chickasaw nations, as follows:

The United States, under a grant especially to be made by the President of the United States, shall cause to be conveyed to the Choctaw Nation a tract of country west of the Mississippi River *in fee simple to them and their descendants*, to inure to them while they shall exist as a nation and live on it * * * (7 Stat. L., p. 333).

Q. Do you mean that means legitimate and illegitimate children?—A. Senator, I do not represent a single person that is illegitimate, but if they are illegitimate children of negro and Indian blood they are, under the decisions of the Department of the Interior, entitled to enrollment as citizens by blood.

Q. Do you mean that it has never been denied that a child of an Indian man and a white woman is entitled to enrollment?—A. Yes.

Q. Whether married or not?—A. Yes.

Q. Is that all covered by your brief?—A. That is all in my brief.

By Mr. Brandegee

Q. Do you claim that the legislation contained in section 4 is void?—A. It raises a unique proposition. It does not say "a person of Indian blood," but it says that unless the records in charge of the Commission show an application, that no name shall be transferred from one roll to another.

Q. Do you claim that that legislation contravenes a treaty?—A. I do.

PATENT ISSUED IN 1842

The patent issued in 1842 under the above treaty conveying the land to the Choctaw Nation contained the identical language used in the treaty.

TREATY OF 1837

In 1837 a treaty was negotiated by and between the Government of the United States and the Choctaw and Chickasaw nations, under which the Chickasaws acquired equal rights in and to the lands then held by the Choctaws under the treaty of 1830. Under this treaty the Chickasaws were to hold the land on the same terms that the Choctaws hold it.

RIGHTS CONFERRED

Now, what rights were conferred upon what persons by the treaty of 1830? That treaty conveyed the lands now being allotted to the members of the Choctaw and Chickasaw nations to the Choctaw Nation in fee simple to them and their descendants. What did this language mean? The Assistant Attorney-General for the Department of the Interior in a test case known as the case of Joe and Dillard Perry, instituted for the purpose of ascertaining and determining the rights of persons of mixed Indian and negro blood, after an elaborated argument and with three of his assistants sitting with him as a court, rendered a decision on February 21, 1905, in which he held

The treaty right referring to the treaty of 1830 was to the Choctaw and Chickasaw nations and their descendants. Descendants is a term of wider significance than heirs or legitimate issue, and includes those springing from an ancestor whether legitimate issue or not.

Mr. McCumber. I notice that the language of the treaty is that the grant is made to the "nation and their descendants." Of course the descendant would be given the construction you give there. But suppose the nation itself, existing as a nation, declares that certain descendants shall not be considered as a part of their nation, would you then consider that this law would be considered to cover their descendants whether they could be valid members or not?—A. The Choctaw and Chickasaw national governments have absolute jurisdiction over those persons that they see fit to admit in their membership. They may admit and expel any of their members. Such has been the decree of the courts. But when a status is fixed by law of Congress or by a treaty with the United States the Choctaw and Chickasaw nations can not disturb that right.

Mr. McCumber. That certain issue shall not become members—issue that is still unborn—would you contend still that they had such a fixed status that the nation could not deal with it?—A. Senator, I most assuredly do. The nation could not, by its own decision, interfere with those rights; but I will come to that in a moment.

Mr. BRANDEGEE. Senator McCumber, as to whether the tribe would not have a right to determine who should constitute its members, I do not think bears upon the question.

Mr. LONG. Has Congress ever sought to determine who were its members?—A. In every Congress act the enrollment of these people has been directed.

Mr. LONG. I want to know whether Congress has ever taken from the tribes the right to determine who were the members of the tribe? Has it ever sought to take from the nation the power to determine who were its members?—A. Only to a limited extent. The Attorney-General holds that where the rights of a person were fixed under a treaty the nation can not divest such person of such right.

That judicial interpretation of the language of the treaty of 1830 has never been modified, changed, or revised, by either the Department of Justice or the Assistant Attorney-General's office or any court of this country in subsequent cases, but on the contrary, it has been strictly adhered to.

And that definition of the word "descendants" is in strict conformity with the definition of every text writer, authority, or judge who has ever attempted to define it.

Descendants, as defined by Bouvier, vol. 1, p. 550, are those who have issued from an individual, including his children, grand children, and their children to the remotest degree. Ambler's Reports, p. 327; 2 Brown's Chancery Cases, ch. 30, p. 230; 1 Roper on Legacies, p. 115.

Thus, under the treaty of 1830, the above-quoted terms of which have never been changed or altered by any subsequent treaty with the United States, or law of Congress, a descendant of a Choctaw was entitled to enjoy the fruits of the grant to an equal degree with any full-blood Choctaw.

The grant thus having been made to the Choctaw Nation and their descendants, Congress could not, even if it saw fit to so do, deprive a person having a right under that treaty of that right, but Congress has never directly attempted to deprive any person of a right fixed by that treaty.

Mr. Justice Gray, in rendering the unanimous opinion of the Supreme Court of the United States in the case of Jones v. Meehan (reported in 175 U. S., p. 1), says:

Congress has no constitutional power to settle the rights under a treaty or to affect titles already granted by a treaty.

Now, if Congress could not change or alter the terms of that grant, could a law enacted by a tribe or an Indian custom change the terms of the grant? I think that no one will seriously so contend. Such power was expressly prohibited by the constitutions of those nations. The Choctaw constitution adopted in 1860 declares:

We, the representatives of the people inhabiting the Choctaw Nation, * * * do mutually agree with each other to form ourselves into a free and independent nation, not inconsistent with the Constitution, treaties, and laws of the United States.

The Chickasaw constitution contains a similar provision. Thus, the legislatures or councils of the two nations could not enact any valid law that even remotely denied a person a property right secured to him under a treaty with, or law of, the United States.

By Mr McCumber

Q Suppose the grant is as you have stated to "a nation and their descendants " afterwards the nation itself passes a law to the effect—assume that this nation has a right to pass a law to the effect—that marriages between members of the nation and colored persons are prohibited and their offspring shall not be members of its tribe nor entitled to any property rights in this tribe you still insist that they would be cut off from passing legislation of that kind and that everybody who would be born from a marriage that would be interdicted must necessarily become a member of the tribe and necessarily entitled to an interest in tribal funds?—A I contend that they could not deprive a person of a property right given such person by treaty with the United States

Q One that may be born ten years from to-day has present property rights?—A I mean to say that property rights attach on the birth of the child The Indian merely enjoys the usufruct of the property up to the time of the distribution of the estate and then takes with all others per capita

Q I claim that no law is intended to cover descendants for all generations, so that a law can be modified that an unborn child in futurity has no property rights that can not be changed by a statute It is granted to the "nation and its descendants " That is, the descendants of the members of the tribe of that nation I do not believe that it was ever intended to be construed to mean that a nation itself, if it exists as a nation, could not prohibit a marriage with a slave and say that those descendants should not become members of the tribe, so that the children of those who have never become members of the nation could still inherit What difference does it make who is a member of a tribe? My position is that the tribe itself can cut off those memberships to the tribe in the future, and that being unborn at the time and not having a right at the time, and their ancestors never becoming a member that is a part of the nation—that the offspring of one who is not a member can not hold under it.

Mr WARNER What legislation has there ever been cutting them off?—A There has never been any legislation cutting them off There is nothing in the Choctaw or Chickasaw constitutions or in the Indian laws that bars these people of their rights

I now come to the treaty of 1866, which has been used by Government officials and the attorneys for the Choctaw and Chickasaw nations for the sole purpose of befogging and obscuring the real issues involved That treaty conferred no property rights upon any one, and does not in the remotest degree conflict with rights given persons under the treaty of 1830 All the treaty of 1866 did was to declare that persons theretofore held in involuntary servitude should be free In addition to this, it provided that if the Choctaw and Chickasaw nations, respectively, within two years from the date or the ratification of the treaty, adopted laws, rules, and regulations giving all persons of African descent, resident in the nations at the date of the treaty of Fort Smith (September 13, 1865), and then descendants, born prior to the ratification of the treaty of 1866 all the rights, privileges, and immunities of any other citizen of said nations, except the right to participate equally in the tribal properties and in lieu thereof gave to each such person and his descendant, theretofore held in slavery, 40 acres of land each, to be held on the same terms as the Choctaws and Chickasaws held it, the Government of the United States would pay to said nations the sum of $300,000 It also provided that if those persons of African descent who were to receive 40 acres of land, in the event that the nations adopted the laws, rules, and regulations giving them this right, saw fit to remove from the nations and relinquish their right to the said 40 acres of land the Government of the United States would pay each of such persons $100

Neither of said nations adopted the requisite laws, rules, and regulations, or any other laws, rules, and regulations within the two years limitation of time provided in the treaty Nor has the Chickasaw Nation at any subsequent time adopted any such laws, rules, and regulations The Choctaw Nation did, however, in 1883 enact laws, rules, and regulations conferring all the rights, privileges, and immunities, including the right of suffrage, on all persons of African descent resident in the Choctaw Nation at the date of the treaty of Fort Smith, and their descendants formerly held in slavery by the Choctaws and Chickasaws, prior to the ratification of the treaty of 1866 Thus, under the laws, rules, and regulations of the Choctaw Nation adopted in conformity with the treaty of 1866 no person of African descent born after the ratification of the treaty of 1866 was entitled to any land whatsoever or to the same rights, privileges, and immunities accorded Choctaw citizens On the contrary, the same act expressly provided that the descendants of these people should be subject to the permit laws of the Choctaw Nation and allowed to remain in the nation during good behavior only

Thus, every allotment of 40 acres of land given to every person of African descent in the Chickasaw Nation, whether he was held in involuntary servitude or not or his descendants, was a pure governmental gratuity Each and every allotment of 40 acres of land given to each and every person of African descent resident in the Choctaw Nation and born after the date of the ratification of the treaty of 1866 has likewise been a pure governmental gratuity, for they had no rights under the treaty of 1866 There is and can be therefore, no conflict between property rights given to persons under the treaty of 1830 and property rights given to persons under laws, rules, and regulations adopted by the Choctaw Nation under and in conformity with the provisions of the treaty of 1866

CONGRESSIONAL ENACTMENTS

We now come to the Congressional enactments designed for the purpose of the extinguishment of the tribal governments and the allotment of the lands of the tribes in severalty Every Congressional enactment, commencing with the act approved March 2, 1889 which created the first Commission to the Five Civilized Tribes, and that has contained any instructions to the Commission relating to the preparation of tribal rolls, has directed the Commission to prepare the rolls in conformity with the treaties and laws with and of the United States Every person enrolled as a Choctaw or Chickasaw citizen by blood to the present day acquired his right to participate in the distribution of the tribal lands and moneys under and by virtue of the treaty of 1830, and not under any acts of Congress or tribal laws or customs

ACT OF JUNE 10, 1896

The first law conferring jurisdiction on the Commission to the Five Civilized Tribes to determine the rights of persons to enrollment as citizens, was the act approved June 10, 1896. That act directed the Commission to receive applications for citizenship in the Choctaw and Chickasaw nations for a period of ninety days after approval thereof, and then gave positive instructions to the Commission how to determine the applications. It provided—

That in determining all such applications said Commission shall respect all of the laws of the several nations or tribes, not inconsistent with the laws of the United States, and all treaties with either of said nations or tribes.

The same act confirmed the then-existing tribal rolls.

Now, what were the powers of the Commission under this act? The Assistant Attorney-General for the Department of the Interior, in a decision rendered March 24, 1905, in the case of Mary Elizabeth Martin, defines the powers of the Commission and the rights of applicants under this law to be—

The Commission had no authority to . . . . deny citizenship to those entitled thereto under treaties and laws with, and of, the United States, or under Indian laws, usages, and customs not inconsistent therewith.

These powers, referring to the powers of the Commission under the above acts, were to admit to citizenship persons whose right was denied or not recognized by the tribal authorities.

Mr. CORNISH. A statement has been made that is so flagrantly incorrect that I want to say a word about it. What is known as the Mary Elizabeth Martin case. That decision was rendered by Attorney-General Campbell. By peremptory order the decision was referred to the Attorney-General of the United States and the decision has been reversed.

Mr. BALLINGER. This interpretation runs through every decision in these cases.

The language of the statute is so plain that it needs no construction by a court. It says exactly what it means and that meaning is clear.

The object of that act was to secure the enrollment of the very class of people we represent and who have been denied their property rights by the Commission and the Department.

ACT OF JUNE 7, 1897

Then followed the act of June 7, 1897, which defined "rolls of citizenship." There having been numerous tribal rolls prepared by different tribal officials of the Choctaw and Chickasaw Nations, at different times, and for various purposes, the question arose as to what particular rolls were confirmed by the act of 1896. The act of 1897 defined them to be—

The last authenticated rolls of each tribe which have been approved by the council of the nation, and the descendants of those appearing on such rolls, and such additional names and their descendants as have been subsequently added. . . .

By operation of this law, as declared by the Assistant Attorney-General for the Department of the Interior, in the case of Mary Elizabeth Martin—

descendants of persons on a confirmed roll were defined and regarded as on the roll where their parents were found, whether themselves actually on such rolls or not, and although born after the rolls were made.

NO ROLLS CONFIRMED.

Inquiry disclosed the fact that the tribal rolls confirmed by the act of June 10, 1896, contained many names fraudulently placed thereon by the tribal authorities. It was discovered that no tribal rolls had been approved by any tribal council as required by the act of June 7, 1897, and therefore no tribal rolls were confirmed by that act.

Only a small percentage of the persons legally entitled to enrollment in the nations had been enrolled by the Commission under the act of 1896. The Choctaw and Chickasaw governmental authorities denied the constitutional power of Congress to prepare tribal rolls and allot lands in severalty; the tribal governments refused the Commission access to the tribal records; the Commission had no power to compel them to deliver up tribal records essential to a proper adjudication of applications for citizenship; in short, the Commission was rendered powerless to prepare correct and complete tribal rolls.

ACT OF JUNE 28, 1898.

Accordingly these facts were reported to Congress by the Commission and the Indian Committee of the House prepared a complete and adequate law clothing the Commission with absolute power to prepare correct tribal rolls, and giving it plenary power to compel all persons having any interest in the Choctaw and Chickasaw nations to appear before it for examination; to subpœna witnesses and to compel them to testify under oath, and to compel the Choctaw and Chickasaw tribal governments to deliver over to the Commission all tribal rolls and records. In fact, the Commission was given every power necessary to the preparation by it of complete and correct tribal rolls, and the act directed it so to do. Here are some of the directions given the Commission under that act:

That in making the rolls of citizenship of the several tribes as required by law. * * * said Commission is authorized and directed to make correct rolls of citizens by blood of all the other tribes, eliminating from the tribal rolls such names as may have been placed thereon by fraud or without authority of law, enrolling such only as may have lawful right thereto and their descendants born since such rolls were made.

Said Commission shall make such rolls descriptive of the persons thereon, so that they may be thereby identified, and it is authorized to take a census of each of said tribes, or to adopt any other means by them deemed necessary to enable them to make such rolls. They shall have access to all rolls and records of the several tribes, and the United States court in Indian Territory shall have jurisdiction to compel the officers of the tribal governments and custodians of such rolls and records to deliver same to said Commission, and on their refusal or failure to do so to punish them as for contempt; as also to require all citizens of said tribes and persons who should be so enrolled to appear before said Commission for enrollment at such times and places as may be fixed by said Commission, and to enforce obedience of all others concerned, so far as the same may be necessary, to enable said Commission to make rolls as herein required, and to punish anyone who may in any manner or by any means obstruct said work.

It shall make a correct roll of all Choctaw freedman entitled to citizenship under the treaties and laws of the Choctaw Nation, and all their descendants born to them since the date of the treaty.

It shall make a correct roll of Chickasaw freedmen entitled to any rights or benefits under the treaty made in 1866 between the United States and the Choctaw and Chickasaw tribes and their descendants born to them since the date of said treaty, and 40 acres of land, including their present residences and improvements, shall be allotted to each, to be selected, held, and used by them until their rights under said treaty shall be determined in such manner as shall hereinafter be provided by Congress.

No person shall be enrolled who has not heretofore removed to and in good faith settled in the nation in which he claims citizenship.

The members of said Commission shall, in performing all duties required of them by law have authority to administer oaths, examine witnesses, and send for persons and papers, and any person who shall willfully and knowingly make any false affidavit or oath to any material fact or matter, before any member of said Commission, or before any other officer authorized to administer oaths to any affidavit or other paper to be filed or oath taken before said Commission, shall be deemed guilty of perjury, and on conviction thereof, shall be punished as for such offenses.

The rolls to be made and approved by the Secretary of the Interior shall be final, and the persons whose names are found thereon with their descendants thereafter born to them with such persons as may intermarry according to tribal laws * * * shall alone constitute the several tribes which they represent.

The Commission under this act was directed to prepare tribal rolls in accordance with the then existing law. The existing law was the treaty of 1830 and the act of 1896 as construed and defined by the act of 1897. The treaty granted lands to the Choctaw Nation and their descendants and the law directed the Commission to accord rights to all persons and their descendants entitled thereto under any treaty with, or law of, the United States.

In every one of these acts we find positive instructions to enroll descendants of all persons entitled to enrollment under any treaties with or laws of the United States.

The Commission did not do that which it was directed to do. It served notice by publication and otherwise upon all persons claiming rights in the Choctaw and Chickasaw nations to appear before it at certain places on certain days. No reference was made in that notice to the making of an application of any kind. The Commission had been instructed by the Department that under the law under which it was then proceeding it could not require nor exact applications of persons claiming rights in the two nations. But in violation of these instructions and the plain language of the statute the Commission compelled every person of mixed Indian and negro blood appearing before it to make an application for the particular kind of citizenship claimed by him. It informed all this class of persons that they could not be enrolled as citizens by blood unless they had been previously recognized by the tribal authorities, which was false.

Q. What do you mean by once he had been recognized by the tribes? A. The Commission construed the appearance of the name of a person on a tribal roll as evidence of his membership in the tribe and informed persons that unless their names appeared on some tribal roll it was useless for them to apply, which was false, the law fixing no such requisite to enrollment by the Commission. This, too, when the Commission had within eight months theretofore informed the Department that no reliance whatever could be placed in tribal rolls prepared by the tribal authorities. It informed the Department that the tribal rolls were loosely kept, any members of the government being at liberty to take them home with him and keep them indefinitely and to loan them to his neighbors, and it was because of this that Congress gave the Commission the power to purge the tribal rolls.

It went further than this, and no persons of mixed Indian and negro blood were permitted to make applications for enrollment as citizens by blood, to which enrollment they were legally entitled, and when such persons appeared before it the Commission arbitrarily

wrote across the top of their examination the words "In the matter
of the application of   for enrollment as a freedman," and so
enrolled them

The Commission was instructed by the Department that in the
preparation of citizenship rolls and freedmen rolls it should compel
each person to appear before it for examination, under oath, his statement to be taken down by the Commission to be subsequently transmitted to the Department when these rolls were sent up for approval
by the Secretary The Commission in the preparation of these rolls
did not regard a single one of the several instructions of the statute
and of the Department Here are some of the records of the examination of these persons

In the matter of the application of Lydia Jackson for enrollment as a Chickasaw
freedman Lydia Jackson enrolled

[Chickasaw freedmen card 281]

REBECCA SAMUELS

I am 28 years old, wife of Parker Samuels, from whom I am separated My mother
is Amanda, daughter of John Kemp I have two children, Ivason Montgomery, aged
12 Bertha Samuels, aged 7 My husband is a United States citizen

PAULS VALLEY September 15, 1898

[Chickasaw freedmen card 672]

DORA M'GEE AND CHILDREN—ANNIE M'GEE

Joe Jackson states that I have a daughter, Dora, 28 wife of Jesse McGee, a Chickasaw They have children Annie, 15 Florence, 11 Mattie, 10 John, 7 Allison, 6,
Wade 4, Ruby 3

ARDMORE September 20, 1898

Mr BALLINGER This case is not dissimilar from the majority of
these cases When Jesse McGee, the father of these children and
the husband of Dora, went before the Commission they would not
let him take with him his wife and children and appear with them
for examination, but they sent him off to the citizenship tent, where
Indians were examined They sent his wife's father off to the freedmen tent to answer questions for his daughter and for these children
Here is the record of their examination and all that was stated
Nine of his children are on the freedmen roll with their mother The
last-born child is on the Indian roll with its father

Why was that last child placed there? The grandfather of these
children was examined by the Commission for them under the law of
1898 The Commission put them on the freedmen roll Under the
act of last year, April 26, 1906, you provided that new-born children
might make application for enrollment, for that kind of enrollment
which they were entitled to Old Jesse McGee had someone make
application for the enrollment of his last-born child, and the Commission was compelled to put it on the roll of citizens by blood

What has been the action of the Indian Office since this question
was raised before the select committee in Indian Territory? I was
informed by the Commissioner the other day that they intended to
take the name of that last child off the citizenship roll Why? He
said there must be uniformity, and because it was easier to take that
name off the citizenship roll where it legally belonged, and put it on
the freedmen roll, where there was no authority of law to place it,
than to take the names of the other children off the freedmen roll and
put them on the citizenship roll, where they are legally entitled to be

[Chickasaw freedman card 557]

EDMUND ROBERTS I am 35 years old and belonged to Carolina Colbert My wife Sarah is 25 and belonged to the Eastmans Children Rachael aged 11 Jamena, aged 7, Charley aged 6 Marcus aged 4 and Lick aged 2 Son of Ned Roberts enrolled

ARDMORE September 20 1898

FREEDMAN

In the matter of the application of Esther Butler to the Commission to the Five Civilized Tribes at Ardmore Ind T April 20 1899 for enrollment as a Choctaw freedman and being duly sworn and examined by Commissioner Needles she testifies as follows

Q What is your name? A Esther Butler
Q How old are you? A I can't tell pretty old
Q Who is your old master? A Peter Pitchlynn
Q Was he a Choctaw or Chickasaw? A He was a Choctaw
Q Have you been living here in the nation all your life? A Yes sir
Q Never went out of it? A No sir I was raised here
Q Got any children living with you? A No sir, I have some grandchildren, though
Q How many? A Three

Enrolled Esther Butler and three grandchildren as Choctaw freedmen

DEPARTMENT OF THE INTERIOR
COMMISSION TO THE FIVE CIVILIZED TRIBES

I hereby certify upon my oath as official oath as stenographer to the above named Commission that the foregoing is a true, full and correct transcription of my stenographic notes

W A SMITH

Can any sane person contend that the examination record in the case of Lydia Jackson sets out any tangible fact upon which her status either as a freedman or an Indian could have been ascertained and determined? All that is contained in the record is

In the matter of the application of Lydia Jackson for enrollment as a Chickasaw freedman Lydia Jackson etc No 5

Mr BRANDLGEE What in fact was her quantum of Indian blood? A As a matter of fact it appears from the record she had very little negro blood the greater quantum, probably 75 per cent. was Indian blood, and she never was held in slavery

Q Under what act do you claim that the Commission was directed, of its own motion to ascertain who ought to go on the rolls? A Under the act of June 28 1898

Mr LONG And disregard tribal rolls entirely? A Disregard everything and put only names on the roll that were entitled to be put on under any treaty with the United States or law of Congress, under any treaty or law of the tribes

As a matter of fact the statements appearing on these records are not the testimony given before the Commission by the persons appearing These records contain merely such portions of the statements made by persons appearing before the Commission as the Commission saw fit to record There is and can be, no possible question as to the correctness of my statements Even where persons attempted to make application for enrollment as citizens by blood their written applications were returned to them with specified instructions that the applications would not be received but if these persons would make applications for enrollment as freedmen the Commission would receive them and so enroll them Here is a sample of the refusal of the Commission to receive the applications of these people

Mr Ballinger When Captain McKennon was before the select committee sitting at McAlester, the question was asked him, "Did you, before these people were enrolled, inquire if they were of Indian blood?" He said, "No, the one thing they were looking for was negro blood."

Mr Brandegee You claim they were not compelled to make any application whatever?—A None whatever, and even when they attempted to comply the Commission absolutely refused

Department of the Interior
Commission to the Five Civilized Tribes,
Muskogee Ind T, *March 16, 1901*

Prince Butler, *Grant, Ind. T*

Dear Sir Receipt is hereby acknowledged of the application for enrollment as a citizen of the Choctaw Nation of George Butler, the infant son of Prince and Mary Butler, born April 3, 1900

The application is again returned for the reason stated in the Commission's letter of the 23d of February The mother of the child appears upon our records as listed for enrollment as a Chickasaw freedman There is inclosed you herewith a new blank application, which you will have made out in conformity with the corrections made in leadpencil upon the application returned you herewith

Upon the return of the new application in proper form for the enrollment of the child as a freedman the matter will be given further consideration

Yours truly

——— ———— *Acting Commissioner*

By Mr Sutherland

Q The effect of that is that the Commission declined to receive an application from this person to be enrolled as a citizen —A Yes, sir, and that refusal now prevents a correction of his erroneous enrollment as a freedman This, nor no other person, was under the act under which he was enrolled, compelled nor authorized to make an application

Q The demand and application should be for enrollment as freedmen?—A When the Commission sent out notice to all persons to come in and appear before it for examination, that notice did not inform these or any other people interested that they would be required to make an application

Mr Brandegee

Q What term did they use in that notice requiring them to come in?—A On July 28, 1898, the notice directed them to appear before the Commission for examination

By Mr McCumber

Q The Commission, as I understand it, took the position that the freedmen were not entitled, under any circumstances, to be enrolled?—A Yes, sir

Q They could not be enrolled as citizens, and therefore there was no necessity of considering their applications?—A Yes, sir

Mr C D Clark

Q Does the law require the Commission to reduce to writing the examination in each case and to show in writing the eligibility of the applicant for enrollment?—A The law directed it to make complete and correct rolls, and gave it the power to subpœna these people and witnesses, and the Department directed it to bring these people before it and examine them under oath and take down their statement in writing

By Mr Long

Q Has Congress ever closed the rolls of this Commission?—A Yes, they were closed in 1902, so far as examination of applicants or the reception of applications were concerned

Q And approved them?—A No, these rolls have not been approved They closed the date for application The adjudication is still going on

By Mr Brandegee

Q They didn't tell them to preserve these statements?—A Yes, sir, in order that the Department might know what the examination was, for the Secretary, under the law had to approve these rolls

Q Do you mean the language of the act of 1898 directed them to preserve the testimony?—A The language of the act does require it The departmental order to the Commission directed them to do this

The Commission knew of the Indian blood and descent of these persons when it arbitrarily enrolled them as freedmen, for on the same day that these examination records were prepared the Commission prepared a field card, which is held by the Commission not to be a part of the confirmed records, on which card appears the name of their Indian parent and his or her enrollment as an Indian (Field card examined)

Mr McCumber:

Q I would like to know if this objection to enrolling them was not pursuant to the Choctaw act of 1883, seventh provision

Be it further enacted That intermarriage with such freedmen of African descent who were formerly held as slaves of the Choctaws and have become citizens, shall not confer any rights of citizenship in this nation and all freedmen who have married or who may hereafter marry freedwomen who have become citizens of the Choctaw Nation are subject to the permit laws and allowed to remain during good behavior only

Was not that the act under which they declined to admit these people?—A That act, like all acts of the Choctaw and Chickasaw nations, was ineffective because it did not prescribe any adequate penalty, or render the children of such marriage illegitimate, the penalty for violation being fifty lashes on the bare back

By Mr Brandegee

Q In the Commission's decision did it cite that paragraph he has read as a basis for its decision?—A No They don't refer to these laws, but they say this is the Indian custom

Q That act is that a marriage shall not confer any property rights?—A It could not deprive a person of tribal rights which he acquired by reason of his Indian blood and descent under the treaty of 1830, for such a law would have been in conflict with the Constitution, laws, and treaties of the United States All the decisions of the Commission were made verbally in the field There are no written decisions to be found

As soon as it was known that the Commission had placed the names of these persons on the freedmen rolls appeal was taken to the Department, and in the first case that reached the Department, which was referred to the Attorney General's Office, the holding of the Commission was reversed, the Department holding that any person of

Choctaw or Chickasaw blood was entitled to enrollment as a citizen by blood, provided only he made an application prior to December 24, 1902. Under this decision of the Department if persons could show by competent testimony that they had applied to the Commission for enrollment as citizens they could secure a correction of their previous erroneous enrollment. Accordingly, the Commissioner, on January 2, 1906, issued the following notice to all persons who claimed they had been erroneously enrolled as freedmen:

In cases of petitioners who do not appear from the records of this office to have formerly applied for enrollment to the Commission to the Five Civilized Tribes as citizens of the Choctaw and Chickasaw nations within the time prescribed by law, the Commission will require conclusive evidence to the effect that application was made or attempted to be made within the time specified for that purpose.

Before this notice was issued the Commissioner had prepared under Departmental instructions a draft of a bill for the purpose of winding up the affairs of the Five Civilized Tribes. The draft prepared by the Commissioner was submitted to the Department of the Interior immediately after the decision in the Joe and Dillard Perry case, establishing their rights, which was in November, 1905. The Secretary appointed a committee composed of officers of the Interior Department to examine the proposed draft of a bill prepared by the Commissioner. That committee supposedly examined the bill and transmitted it to the Secretary, with a supposedly explanatory report. The Secretary of the Interior examined the bill also, as he stated in his communication of transmittal. Says he:

I have carefully examined the provisions of said bill and earnestly recommend that the matter receive early and favorable consideration by Congress.

In that bill was section 4, about which so much complaint has been made. No man on this committee knew the object sought to be accomplished by that section or its evil results, and careful pains were taken that every member of this committee should remain in ignorance. The section itself appeared innocent enough. It provided:

Sec. 4. That no name shall be transferred from the approved freedmen, or any other approved rolls of the Choctaw, Chickasaw, Cherokee, Creek, or Seminole tribes, respectively, to the roll of citizens by blood, unless the records in charge of the Commissioner to the Five Civilized Tribes show that application for enrollment as a citizen by blood was made within the time prescribed by law by or for the party seeking the transfer, and said records shall be conclusive evidence as to the fact of such application, unless it be shown by documentary evidence that the Commission to the Five Civilized Tribes actually received such application within the time prescribed by law.

By Mr. Long:

Q. Section 4, as it was prepared by the Interior Department and transmitted to Congress, did not contain the last few lines?—A. No, sir; it did not.

Q. That was put in at your suggestion?—A. Yes, sir.

Mr. McCumber. And with regard to the words "record evidence" and "documentary evidence?"—A. That is in the last amendment.

Mr. Brandegee. Do you claim that up to the time of the passage of section 4, which made the records of the Commission conclusive upon the question of an application, unless documentary evidence is offered that these people could be and were entitled to, under the law, enrollment as citizens by blood?—A. Yes, Senator. Until Congress enacted section 4 they were all entitled to show by competent evidence that they attempted to assert their right to enrollment as citizens by blood when before the Commission at any time between June 10, 1896, to December 25, 1902. Although the law under which they were enrolled did not require any application or assertion of right of any kind—the Commission being directed to ascertain this—and upon proof that they did make an assertion of right as Indians they could have their names transferred from the freedmen roll to the roll of citizens by blood, provided the Commission and the Department would consider the case.

Mr. LONG. When were the rolls closed?—A. No examinations or applications could be conducted or received after December 25, 1902.

Mr. BALLINGER. I think that it can be clearly shown—I have attempted to do so—that there is no decision of any Department or court that deprives these people of their rights because of lack of Indian blood. That they are citizens of these nations there is no question, and the only thing that has barred them has been the illegal holding of the Commission and illegal acts of the Commission. If the Commission had made a record of their applications, made a record of their Indian blood, we would not be here to-day.

In its report the committee pretended to give an explanation of the provisions of section 4. Here is what that committee said of section 4:

Section 4 prohibits the transfer of a name from the approved freedmen or other rolls of said tribes to the roll of citizens of blood unless application for enrollment as citizen by blood was made within the time prescribed by law.

This explanation could not have been intended to explain. If the committee had designedly prepared a statement for the sole purpose of concealing the object sought by section 4 it could not have drafted a more adroit statement than the one submitted. The statement did not even set out the requirements of the section; it did not state that at the time the class of persons with which it was dealing were examined by the Commission; that there was no authority or law to compel or require them to make an application, and if they made an application for enrollment it was of no force and effect under the statute under which they were enrolled; it did not state that the records which were made conclusive were absolutely silent as to any assertion of right to enrollment as a citizen by blood; it did not state that the Commission while in the field disregarded the instructions of the Department and did not make a record of the actual testimony of the applicants; it did not state that if section 4 was enacted into law it would deprive 1,500 persons who were, under the treaties and laws with and of the United States, entitled to enrollment as Indians by reason of their descent, blood, and residence, to such enrollment; it did not state the rights of these persons to have their names transferred from the freedmen roll to the roll of citizens by blood had been judicially ascertained by the Department less than thirty days before the transmission of the report to Congress; it did not state these and numerous other well-known facts pertinent to an intelligent understanding of this question. But both the committee and the Secretary stated that they had made a thorough investigation of this section and the Secretary earnestly recommended that the bill with this section in it receive early and favorable consideration.

That section was enacted into law, and what has been the result? Not one single name of a person on the freedman roll has been transferred to the roll of citizens by blood. The first case referred to the Assistant Attorney-General under section 4 was the case of the children of Katie Wilson who were the children of a recognized and enrolled Choctaw citizen by blood After reviewing the Indian blood and descent of these children and stating that they were enrolled by the Commission under the act of 1898, the Assistant Attorney-General says

All this however, is immaterial in view of the provisions of section 4 of the act approved April 26 1906
Under the facts stated by the Commissioner these applicants come clearly within the inhibition of this provision of law and their request to be transferred can not be granted It is not claimed in the papers now before me that application for enrollment as a citizen by blood was made within the time prescribed by law by or for any of these persons, nor is there anything to indicate that any of them come within the exception in the law In other words there is nothing tending to impugn the correctness of the statement that no such application was made
The law prohibits the transfer of these names and the application must for that reason be denied
It is not intended by this to express any opinion as to the merits of the case or as to what action would have been proper in the absence of a provision like that of the act of April 26, 1906

Both the Commission and the Department have resorted to every technicality known to them to deprive these applicants of any rights which they have even under section 4

In the case of Calvin Newberry et al the Commissioner held that where an application was made to the Commission in 1906, and appears of record on the dockets of the Commission, but which was subsequently transferred by order of the United States court of the southern district of Indian Territory to said court and which has never been actually returned to the Commission, that as the application is not actually in the custody of the Commissioner the party is barred from securing a transfer of his name and the names of his children under section 4 The Indian Office affirmed less than thirty days ago the holding of the Commissioner in this case

This is a fair illustration of the absurd technicalities employed by the Commissioner and the Department to defeat the rights of these parties

The Commissioner and the Department have for the past six months invoked a decision approved pro forma by the Secretary, and which was written by a man insane at the time he prepared the decision, and who was within a few days thereafter adjudged by the supreme court of the District of Columbia to be insane, and by its decree incarcerated in the insane asylum across the river, and who has since died in the insane asylum, to defeat rights not defeated by section 4 The decision prepared by this lunatic decided questions not in the record, and not before the Department in that case for decision, on mere technicalities with reference to the making of an application and did not refer to the merits of the case

This decision now being strictly adhered to by the Commissioner and the Department is diametrically opposite to every decision rendered by the Assistant Attorney-General for the Department of the Interior and the Attorney-General of the United States in these cases This would be grotesque were it not for the fact that persons are being deprived of property rights by adherence thereto

Mr McCumber He married a negro woman His children appear on the 1895 census roll?—A I presume the general custom followed was the reverse, but the Choctaw and Chickasaw nations have done all kinds of funny things

It is because of these facts that we are pleading for mandatory legislation that will leave no discretion whatever with either the Commissioner or the Department in the determination of this class of cases.

RIGHTS OF APPLICANTS RECOGNIZED BY TRIBAL LAWS.

It has been contended by both the Commissioner and the attorneys for the nations that persons of mixed Indian and negro blood had no right under tribal laws, customs, and usages, and therefore they are barred from participating in the distribution of the tribal property. Every adult male person of this class is and ever has been, under the Choctaw and Chickasaw constitutions, eligible to hold any office from principal chief down to the lowest office under the tribal government. The constitutions of the Choctaw and Chickasaw nations prescribe the qualifications to hold high office to be: (1) A free male citizen; (2) a lineal descendant of the Choctaw or Chickasaw race; (3) residence in the nation.

Is it possible that a person is eligible to hold any office in a nation and is not a citizen of that nation?

It has been contended by the Commissioner and the attorneys for the nation that some of these persons are illegitimate. That we deny, and assert that they are each and every one legitimate; that their legitimacy has been declared by the courts of the country. In the case of Wall v. Williamson (11 Alabama, 839), which was a Choctaw case, it was held that the mere living together of a Choctaw man and woman constituted a valid marriage, and that the abandonment of the woman by the man constituted a valid divorce, and that the children were legitimate.

In this case the testimony showed conclusively that such was the custom of the Choctaw Nation, and it is well known to every person familiar with conditions in the Choctaw and Chickasaw nations that this was the custom down to the time the Commission began its work. In the case of Wall v. Williamson, reported in the eighth Alabama reports, the court says, in referring to the tribal laws and customs relating to and controlling marriage and divorce among the Choctaws:

Whatever may have been the capacity of the husband to abandon his wife, and thereby to dissolve the marriage if both had become residents of Alabama, after the tribe had departed from its limits, it is very clear that the same effect must be given to a dissolution of the marriage by the Choctaw law as given to the marriage by the same law. By that law it appears the husband may at pleasure dissolve the relation. His abandonment is evidence that he has done so. We conceive the same effect must be given to this act as would be given a lawful decree in a civilized community dissolving the marriage. However strange it may appear, at this day, that a marriage may thus easily be dissolved, the Choctaws are scarcely worse than the Romans, who permitted the husband to dismiss his wife for the most frivolous causes. (Story, Confl. of Laws, 169.)

This decision was adopted by the supreme court of the State of Missouri in determining a similar question and the same general proposition has been adhered to by many other State courts, there being no exceptions that we have been able to find.

Many of these persons were legally and lawfully married under the laws of the United States, and many more were legally and lawfully married under the laws of the Choctaw Nation, but the records of their marriages can not now be produced because no records were kept. If by their failure to produce these marriage certificates their children are rendered illegitimate, then the great majority of the people of the Choctaw and Chickasaw nations are illegitimate, for they can not produce marriage certificates or court records, and but few even know the import of a marriage license.

Laws were enacted by the Choctaw and Chickasaw nations purporting to regulate marriage and divorce, but each and every enactment is deficient and lacking in all the essentials of a positive law. No penalties are prescribed for violation of the laws. It is not provided that a marriage contracted contrary to the terms of the law shall be invalid or the children born of such a marriage shall be illegitimate. It is not provided that a divorce procured other than prescribed in the statute shall be void, and the Choctaw and Chickasaw people have treated those laws as a dead letter, wholly disregarding them, and continued their social relations under the former tribal customs.

But if everyone of these persons is illegitimate, as has been so strenuously contended by both the Commissioner and the attorneys for the nation, and which will probably be insisted to-day, they would still be entitled to enrollment as citizens by blood of the Choctaw and Chickasaw nations if the Commission had performed its duty under the act of June 28, 1898, and had placed in the examination records a statement of their Indian blood and descent, and the actual statements made by them when examined.

This is not to bare assertion of counsel. It is the finding of the Assistant Attorney-General for the Department of the Interior, the highest tribunal authorized by law to pass upon their rights. Here is what he says of their rights in an opinion rendered February 21, 1905, affirmed in an opinion rendered November 11, 1905, and reaffirmed September 26, 1906:

The treaty right (referring to the treaty of 1830) was to the Choctaw and Chickasaw nations and their descendants. Descendants, as pointed out in the case of James W. Shirley, is a term of wider significance than heirs, or legitimate issue, and includes those springing from an ancestor whether legitimate issue or not. The descent of the applicants is fully and indubitably shown to be from Charles Perry, a Chickasaw by blood, recognized by him and born of a union that he and Eliza evidently regarded as a lawful one, openly avowed and by the Chickasaw Nation tolerated, which it did not compel him to abandon or impose the penalties of its laws upon him for contracting and observing. The law properly enough imposed no penalty or contamination of blood upon the innocent issue of such a union. I am therefore clearly of the opinion that the applicants are entitled to be transferred to the roll of Chickasaws by blood.

Q. When was that decision?—A. The third one was September 26, 1906. The second, November 11, 1905. The first one was rendered February 21, 1905.

By Mr. BRANDEGEE:

Q. November 11, 1905, the Joe and Dillard Perry case was decided, under which decision, if it had been under the act of 1906, which we adopted, these people would not have been on the roll?—A. No, sir.

Q. In the decision of that case—the second decision—that under this act of July 1, 1902, the rolls having been closed they were not entitled to be considered. Then you produced some additional evidence showing that they had made application before that?—A. The second decision was that if they had not been able to establish by competent evidence that they had made application prior to December 24, 1902, and as they could not establish that by competent evidence they were barred. Then it was subsequently found that they had made an application in writing to the Commission and that it was on file, and that that application had not been certified up as a part of the record in that case. Then came the third decision, of September 26, 1906, in which they were ordered to be enrolled.

By Mr. BRANDEGEE:

Q. It was a continuing application?—A. Yes, sir.

By Mr. WARNER:

Q. At what time is it necessary to show that an application was made?—A. Any time between June 10, 1896, down to the 25th day of December, 1902.

Q. Most of these children are children of Indian fathers and negro mothers?—A. The majority of them are.

Q. Are there any exceptions?—A. Yes. There are instances where the offspring is of an Indian woman and negro man.

By Mr. C. D. CLARK:

Q. In other words, where the negro blood comes from the father?—A. Yes, sir.

Q. What was the holding of the Commission?—A. In substance this. That where any person had a strain of negro blood in them descending from an ancestor once held in involuntary servitude that the servile blood contaminated and polluted the Indian blood and render such person incapable of taking land under a treaty with the United States.

By Mr. LONG:

Q. The Commission followed the rule followed by the tribe?—A. No, sir.

Q. It was the rule under which the tribal rolls were always constructed, was it not?—A. No, sir.

By Mr. BRANDEGEE:

Q. What had been the tribal law?—A. There is no tribal law.

Q. Tribal custom then. They had the tribal rolls as a basis?—A. I can not answer that.

Q. Is it not a fact that the tribes did follow the laws of the Southern States at the time the tribes held these slaves?—A. In many cases where a person was liberated, for instance, in 1860 they were adopted into the nation.

By Mr. LONG:

Q. When the Commission holds the other way they are following what before the war had been the custom of these tribes of Indians. Does the same follow here?—A. I can not say what the tribal custom was.

Q. I am speaking of the custom of making up the rolls of the tribe. The roll of negroes and the descendants of mixed blood, where there is no special legislation, how they come to make up their rolls?—A. The Choctaws appointed committees to go out and prepare tribal rolls.

Q. On what theory would those committees act when they came to a person of mixed blood?—A. In many instances they enrolled them as citizens and their names appear on the tribal rolls.

By Mr. C. D. CLARK:

Q. I understand that these rolls that had been prepared by the tribe—the correctness of them is now disputed, both by the Commissioner and the Five Civilized Tribes?—A. By the tribes themselves. Yes, sir; that is a fact.

Q. And the dispute is made because the rolls had been imperfectly made?—A. They were very careless and the officials corrupt in making up the rolls.

Q. In other words, that both the tribes and the Commissioner did dispute them and do dispute now the correctness of the tribal rolls?—A. Yes, sir; notwithstanding that fact, they insist upon adhering to those rolls as a basis for citizenship.

Q. Did the Commission misconstrue the law when they took these rolls as a basis?—A. Under the act of 1898 the Commission was authorized to disregard any tribal rolls.

Q. What did the Commission do. Did they disregard all rolls and make one of their own?—A. Certainly. There were many full bloods down there that were not on any tribal roll.

By Mr. BRANDEGEE:

Q. New names were added?—A. Yes, sir.

Q. And old names were stricken off?—A. Yes, sir.

Q. Did the Commission make a new roll, disregarding the rolls of the tribe?—A. Yes, sir.

It has never been contended by the Commissioner or the Department that an illegitimate child begotten by an Indian man on a white woman, or on a woman of any other race or nationality other than a negro, was not entitled to enrollment as a Choctaw or Chickasaw citizen by blood. We contend that a child begotten on a negro woman is entitled to equal rights. It has never been held by the Commissioner or the Department that a child of one part Indian blood and thirty-one parts white blood, whose father or mother was a member of the Choctaw or Chickasaw nations was not entitled to enrollment as a citizen by blood. We respectfully contend that if such is the case that certainly a child of a recognized Indian mother or father, possessed of a greater quantum of Indian blood, although of negro descent on one side, is equally entitled to recognition.

We respectfully contend that these persons are Choctaw and Chickasaw citizens by blood; that they are lineal descendants by blood of the identical persons to whom the grant was originally made; that they acquired their citizenship in the Choctaw and Chickasaw nations by descent from recognized citizens by blood thereof, by birth in the nations, and by continuous and uninterrupted residence therein and allegiance thereto. These are the essential elements of citizenship, for can it be denied that the child of a recognized citizen of a nation, born in the nation, and owing its allegiance to that nation and to no other, is a stranger to its parents' allegiance and parents' citizenship? This is the fundamental and universal law of all organized societies and States and essential to their continued existence as such. In no State and by no government has it ever been held that the offspring of a citizen is a born stranger to the parents' allegiance, outcast from the parents' civil state and citizen of no other State. Such was not the law of the Choctaw Nation as declared by the chief justice of the supreme court of the Choctaw Nation.

I will now show you from a decision of the supreme court of the Choctaw Nation that the birth of a child to a recognized and enrolled parent conferred upon the child full citizenship, and that the enrollment of an ancestor carried with it the enrollment of his descendants

Wm Buckholts was admitted to Choctaw citizenship by the supreme court of the Choctaw Nation in 1872, under act of the Choctaw Nation of March 20, 1872

Buckholts asked the court to include in the judgment admitting him to citizenship "the names of his descendants, but was informed by the chief justice that this was unnecessary, and that his recognition as a Choctaw by blood carried with it the recognition of his children A judge of the court testified that such was the custom of the court

The Commission to the Five Civilized Tribes enrolled the descendants of Wm Buckholts under the act of June 28, 1898

The attorneys for the Choctaw Nation protested against the enrollment of Buckholts' descendants by the Commission on the ground that the father of these descendants, and son of Wm Buckholts was living at the time of his father's admission by the court, and the court not having included his name in the judgment, he could acquire no Choctaw citizenship by virtue of the admission of his father

Held by the Assistant Attorney-General "The supreme court certainly had jurisdiction to construe and announce the effect and force of its decree and to conclude the Choctaw Nation by such interpretation of its law "

By Mr BRANDEGEE

Q Is this the pith of your claim or not, that although in effect these freedmen that you represent, or some of them, did apply in the field for enrollment, and that there is no record in the Commissioner's office that any such application was made? A Yes, sir

Q And that that being so they are barred by the language of this act of ours? Where that is so, there has got to be documentary evidence that they made application? A Yes, sir

Q And the Commission failed to preserve the application?—A Yes, sir

Q And that these people did make application? A Yes, sir

Q Coupled with this legislation we passed last year, these people are barred from what would be their rights but for that? A Yes, sir

---

COMMITTEE ON INDIAN AFFAIRS,
UNITED STATES SENATE,
Washington, D C, January 24, 1907

The committee met at 10 o'clock a m

Present Senators Clapp (chairman), McCumber, Clark of Wyoming; Long, Warner, Sutherland, Brandegee, La Follette, Dubois, Clark, of Montana; Teller, and Stone

The CHAIRMAN Mr Cornish, you may proceed

Mr CORNISH Mr Chairman and gentlemen of the committee, I shall address myself to the question presented by Mr Ballinger, as to the right of certain persons heretofore enrolled as freedmen and alleged to be of mixed negro and Indian blood and entitled to be enrolled, not as freedmen, but as Choctaw and Chickasaw Indians

I am not insensible of the responsibility that rests upon me as one of the representatives of the Choctaws and Chickasaws to so place this matter before your committee that you will intelligently grasp the issues presented and be able to justly and fairly pass upon those issues and do that which will be right and lawful in the premises. The responsibility not only rests upon us as representatives of the tribes, but on you as representatives of the great Government of the United States, the guardian and protector of the property of these Indian tribes.

This proposition is a new one, and in all of the matters which have been presented to your committee for the past ten years, or since the Government of the United States began its administration of citizenship for the tribes, it has never been heard of until within a less time than two years ago. If these contentions should be established and you should feel that this act which is proposed (and which would be in violation of every custom and usage of the tribes, as well as every law of the Government of the United States and every decision of every tribunal of the Government of the United States) should be taken it would mean the taking away from the Choctaws and Chickasaws of property to the value of many millions of dollars. It would be revolutionary as to the work of the Government and would upset its work in citizenship matters for the past ten years.

Now, as a first proposition, it is asked that this proposed action, if taken, be based upon a construction of the word "descendants" contained in the treaty of 1830. It is maintained that if it can be shown that a particular individual person is the physical progeny of an Indian man that he becomes such a descendant as, within the meaning of the treaty of 1830, would make him entitled to participate in the distribution of the tribal property of the Choctaws and the Chickasaws and to receive property as an individual of the value of from $5,000 to $10,000.

Senator CLARK, of Wyoming. Is that the estimated value of each one of those shares?

Mr. CORNISH. Yes, sir; that is the estimated value of an allotment in the Choctaw and Chickasaw nations—from $5,000 to $10,000. It is 320 acres of land, and in addition to that there will be another allotment of land, and also participation in the moneys of the tribes.

Senator LONG. Did you say 320 acres of land?

Mr. CORNISH. Yes, sir; an average of 320. If it is poorer land it means a greater number of acres, and if it is richer land it may be 160 acres.

I suggest, as I have already stated, that the magnitude of the subject requires that the Congress of the United States and this committee should certainly move with great deliberation and very slowly before upsetting everything that has been done by the tribes for generations, and everything which has been done by the Government of the United States in the administration of these matters, and under the laws provided by Congress.

Now, I return to a discussion of the word "descendants." Gentlemen, I do not believe that the representatives of the Government of the United States and the representatives of the Indians meant that the use of the word "descendant" in the treaty of 1830 had the meaning contended for. If you should pass a law at this time it is not reasonable to suppose that you would give that meaning to the use of that word. I believe the use of the word "descendants," as used in the treaty of 1830, if it stood alone, and if we could look only to that word itself (and we can not look only to that word, as I will show you a little later on, because whatever meaning that word may have in that treaty is modified, and a flood of light is thrown on its meaning by an examination of the later treaties) was intended to have a natural, usual, and reasonable meaning. It is upon the construction of that word that the whole matter is based. I believe that those representatives at that time intended to give to that word the meaning which you generally would give to the word if you were using it at this time. I do not believe, in view of conditions as they exist at this time, that this committee and this Congress would make use of that word "descendants," in referring to those who were members of the Choctaw and the Chickasaw nations, in such a way as to confer property rights upon an individual who is the illegitimate child of an Indian man and any kind of a woman, whether negro or white woman.

Senator BRANDEGEE. Who are the negotiators of that treaty?

Mr CORNISH. Gen. John Coffey was, I believe, the representative of the Government of the United States; he was the commissioner upon the ground. Of course it was afterwards debated and ratified by Congress, but he was the commissioner who preliminarily negotiated the treaty.

Now, in order to establish the point which I am now considering, conceding that those persons are the physical progeny of an Indian man—and we do not concede that—but conceding the fact that these 1,000 or 1,500 persons who are now asking property rights at the hands of this committee and this Congress were begotten by Indian men and are the physical progeny of Indian men upon negro women, or other women for that matter, and therefore illegal and illegitimate children, I do not believe that this committee would give that word "descendants" such a definition as would violate every law, custom, and usage of the tribes and be at variance with the law of the land.

Senator SUTHERLAND. Is it your idea that the word "descendants" is used there in the sense of heirs?

Mr CORNISH. I think it would be unprofitable for us to look for an academic definition of the word "descendants" and I do not believe that the rights of Chickasaw and Choctaw citizenship should be conferred or were intended to be conferred upon persons situated as those persons were situated. Yes; I will answer your question affirmatively.

Now, gentlemen, I stated that an examination of the later treaties throws a flood of light upon the use of that word in that treaty, and when we examine the later treaties it develops, I think, conclusively that we can not look to the word "descendant" as used in the treaty of 1830 to determine who are to share, or what classes are to share, in the distribution.

The language of the second article of the treaty of 1830, as contended by counsel for claimants, is as follows:

* * * The United States, under a grant specially to be made by the President of the United States, shall cause to be conveyed to the Choctaw Nation a tract of country west of the Mississippi River, in fee simple, to them and their descendants, to insure to them while they shall exist as a nation and live upon it * * * (and then follows the description).

It is also true that it is provided by the first article of the treaty of 1837, under which the Chickasaws purchased an interest in these lands, that—

It is agreed by the Choctaws that the Chickasaws shall have the privilege of forming a district within the limits of their country, to be held on the same terms that the Choctaws now hold it   *   *   *

They, however, overlook entirely the treaty of 1855 and the circumstances which rendered it necessary

These fully appear from an examination of the treaty itself

Its preamble is as follows:

Whereas the political connections heretofore existing between the Choctaw and Chickasaw tribes of Indians have given rise to unhappy and injurious dissensions and controversies among them, which renders necessary a readjustment of their relations to each other and to the United States, and whereas the United States desire that the Choctaw Indians shall relinquish all claim to any territory west of the one hundredth degree of west longitude and also to make provision for the permanent settlement within the Choctaw country of the Wichita and certain other tribes or bands of Indians, for which purpose the Choctaws and Chickasaws are willing to lease, on reasonable terms, to the United States that portion of their common territory which is west of the ninety-eighth degree of west longitude and whereas the Choctaws contend that by a just and fair construction of the treaty of September 27, 1830, they are of right entitled to the net proceeds of the land ceded by them to the United States under said treaty, and have proposed that the question of their right to the same, together with the whole subject-matter of their unsettled claims, whether national or individual against the United States arising under the various provisions of said treaty, shall be referred to the Senate of the United States for final adjudication and adjustment, and whereas it is necessary, for the simplification and better understanding of the relations between the United States and the Choctaw Indians, that all their subsisting treaty stipulations be embodied in one comprehensive instrument

Now, therefore, the United States of America, by their commissioner, George W Manypenny, the Choctaws, by their commissioners Peter P Pitchlynn Israel Fulsom, Samuel Garland, and Dixon W Lewis and the Chickasaws, by their commissioners, Edmund Pickens and Sampson Folsom, do hereby agree and stipulate, as follows

ARTICLE 1

The following shall constitute and remain the boundaries of the Choctaw and Chickasaw country (and then the description)

And pursuant to an act of Congress approved May 28, 1830, the United States do forever secure and guarantee the lands embraced within said limits to the members of the Choctaw and Chickasaw tribes their heirs and successors, to be held in common, so that each and every member of either tribe shall have an equal undivided interest in the whole provided, however no part thereof shall ever be sold without the consent of both tribes and that said lands shall revert to the United States if said Indians and their heirs become extinct or abandon the same

It is also provided by article 21 of this agreement, as follows

This convention shall supersede and take the place of all former treaties between the United States and the Choctaws and also all treaty stipulations between the United States and the Chickasaws and between the Choctaws and Chickasaws inconsistent with this agreement   *   *   *

That the treaty of 1855, above quoted, is the basis of the title of the Choctaws and Chickasaws to their lands, and fixes the terms upon which it is held, is reflected in the treaty of 1866, article 11 of which is as follows

Whereas the land occupied by the Choctaw and Chickasaw nations, and described in the treaty between the United States and said nations of June 22 1855, is now held by the members of said nations, in common under the provisions of said treaty   *   *   *

If, as contended, the word "descendants," as used in the treaty of 1830, when abstractly and academically considered, should be held to mean physical progeny, such a definition, however unjust and unreasonable it may be, can have no application to the lands of the Choctaws and Chickasaws and the terms and conditions under which they are held, for it is expressly agreed by all the contracting parties and the parties in interest (the United States and the Choctaws and Chickasaws) that the former treaties fixing the rights of the parties were unsatisfactory to all, and that they should be abrogated and set aside and that

* * * it is necessary for the simplification and better understanding of the relations between the United States and the Choctaw Indians that all their subsisting treaty stipulations be embodied in one comprehensive instrument * * *

And then follows article 1 of the treaty of 1855, providing that the lands referred to are guaranteed to the

* * * members of the Choctaw and Chickasaw tribes, their heirs and successors, * * *

and also that said lands shall revert to the United States if

* * * said Indians and their heirs

become extinct or abandon the same

No trouble is encountered in disposing of the contention of the present applicants when the facts in their cases are considered in the light of the definition of the terms heirs and successors contained in the law books

Now we come to the treaty of 1898 The committee will understand that the treaty of 1898 is the basic law upon which the Government of the United States is proceeding at this time for the purpose of settling citizenship and dividing tribal property

Now, in the law of 1898 and later laws and treaties amending the same, is contained the authority by which the representatives of the Government of the United States can determine who are the citizens of the tribes, and how they shall participate in the tribal property of the Choctaws and Chickasaws

Senator LONG That is the Curtis Act?

Mr CORNISH Yes sir the act of June 28, 1898

Senator LONG What section?

Mr CORNISH I have reference now to section 16 After providing how the rolls of the Cherokee and Creek nations shall be made, it is provided as follows

Said Commission is authorized and directed to make correct rolls of the citizens by blood of all the other tribes eliminating from the tribal rolls such names as have been placed thereon by fraud or without authority of law enrolling such only as may have lawful right thereto and their descendants born since such rolls were made, with such intermarried white persons as may be entitled to Choctaw and Chickasaw citizenship under the treaties and laws of said tribe

Mr BALLINGER The first provision of that section that you have just read provides that the rolls shall be made in accordance with existing law?

Mr CORNISH Yes Now, gentlemen, this law, and the later laws to which I shall shortly refer provides in terms that there is no power in any tribunal or any representative of the Government of the United States to enroll any person who does not appear upon some one of the tribal rolls of the Choctaw and Chickasaw nations The Government of the United States in making up those rolls and in determining who are to participate in tribal property is to be limited in its jurisdiction and in the jurisdiction of its tribunals by what the tribes themselves have done in pursuance of their laws, customs, and usages.

Senator LONG. Is it your contention that the Commission could take names off but could not put names on?

Mr. CORNISH. Exactly; that is exactly what I am coming to. Now, gentlemen, if there are any persons in this world who have condemned the Choctaw and Chickasaw rolls and the acts of the Choctaws and Chickasaws—the Indian themselves—in citizenship matters, it has been their own attorneys. We are aware, in the conduct of our work, and in the efforts which we have made from the year 1899 to the present time to get these matters in such condition as that the property of our clients would be protected and the good name of the Government of the United States would be left unstained—in the pursuit of that work we have discovered a condition which is conceded by all, that the tribes themselves have not done as they should have done in the making up of their citizenship rolls; and that is one of the strongest arguments that has been made before Congress and the Commission of the Five Civilized Tribes, as well as the other tribunals of the Government of the United States in support of our contention from the beginning. But the fault was not in refusing enrollment to worthy applicants, but the fault was in the wrongful admission of hundreds and thousands of unworthy persons by acts of the tribal councils and by fraudulent and corrupt acts of their own officials in making up those rolls. It is perhaps not in order for me to give instances of how persons claiming some strain of Indian blood, by arrangement with some tribal officials who had influence with the council, or who had influence with the enrolling Commission, would bring about the placing of their names on tribal rolls wrongfully, and in many instances corruptly, for a consideration, and for various other reasons. That has been established, and is well known. The fault, if there was a fault, was in placing many persons upon those tribal rolls who were unworthy and not entitled, but who could enlist improper though effective influences. The tribes rarely ever denied enrollment to any persons entitled, but the fault was in placing upon the rolls many hundreds of persons who were not entitled, through corrupt influences. That is a matter of history. The proper inquiry is as to what is the law at this time, in determining who are citizens and entitled to enrollment and allotment. I state that under the laws of 1898 and 1900 and the treaty of 1902 (ratifying the two former acts) that the Government has no power to enroll any person who has not been enrolled by the tribes, and the descendants of such persons born since such enrollment.

Throughout this whole discussion I shall exclude all reference to Mississippi Choctaws, as their rights are in nowise involved. I say that the limit of the jurisdiction of the Government of the United States and its tribunals to place upon the final rolls being made at this time by your authority, the limit of that jurisdiction is the tribal rolls made by the tribes themselves.

Senator BRANDEGEE. May I ask you a question there? Inasmuch as that is the basis of your whole claim, and as that was Mr. Ballinger's claim, I would like to ask you, then—if it is so, as I understand you, that you agree with Mr. Ballinger's statement that the first article of that treaty compels them to take into consideration the other treaties of the United States—how is it that you claim that the United States has limited its tribunals in the adjudication of these Indian matters solely and alone to the customs of the tribe?

Mr Cornish I am coming to that. I will make that plain I have read to the committee that part of section 16 of the act of June 28, 1898, which is part of the Atoka Agreement, which provides how the rolls shall be made

Senator McCumber Won't you please read it again?

Mr Cornish It is as follows

Said Commission is authorized and directed—

I should say that there was a special provision as to the Creek roll and certain special provisions as to the Cherokee roll This is the general provision under which the rolls are to be made—

Said Commission is authorized and directed to make correct rolls of the citizens by blood of all the other tribes eliminating from the tribal rolls such names as may have been placed thereon by fraud or without authority of law enrolling such as may have lawful right thereto and their descendants born since such rolls were made with such intermarried white persons as may be entitled to Choctaw and Chickasaw citizenship under the treaties and the laws of said tribes

Now, when the Commission of the Five Civilized Tribes began its work under that law in the fall of 1898, it held a series of appointments, it made a camping trip through the Chickasaw Nation for the purpose of receiving applications of the Choctaw and Chickasaw Indians and the Choctaw and Chickasaw freedmen under the provisions of that law

Senator McCumber That law provides for eliminating such as were improperly on the rolls, and the enrolling of those that belonged on the rolls Do you claim that under that you should give force only to the elimination provision and not to the others?

Mr Cornish Exactly I will make myself perfectly plain on that subject as I proceed

When the Commission began its work the people who are now in that country to the extent of many thousands, and who have sworn that they are the descendants of some particular Choctaw or Chickasaw Indian, began to insist before the Commission that it should not only receive the applications of persons whose names were upon some one of the tribal rolls, but that it should receive the application and pass upon that application upon its merits, of every man, woman, and child who was willing to swear that he was the descendant of a Choctaw Indian, without any limitation

That question perplexed the Commission, and the question of law involved was submitted to the then Assistant Attorney-General of the Interior Department, Mr Willis Van Devanter a gentleman who is known for his ability as a lawyer by perhaps every member of this committee That particular inquiry was submitted to Mr Van Devanter, the Assistant Attorney-General for the Interior Department, on March 17, 1899, as to whether or not there was any power in the Commission to receive the application of any person unless the name of that person was upon some one of the tribal rolls of the Choctaw and Chickasaw nations Mr Van Devanter considered all the laws that had been passed prior to that time, and on March 17, 1899, he rendered a most comprehensive opinion, which holds, in terms, that tary's jurisdiction in his power over the Commission was fixed by the

the limit of the Commission's jurisdiction, and the limit of the Secretribal rolls which had been made by the tribes themselves. I have a copy of that opinion and ask that so much of it as bears upon this contention be made a part of my remarks. It is as follows:

"The act of June 28. 1898, supra, prescribes the manner in which the commission is to make rolls of citizenship of tne several tribes, and that all names found to have been placed upon the tribal rolls by fraud or without authority of law shall be eliminated, and then declares:

"The rolls so made, when approved by the Secretary of the Interior, shall be final, and the persons whose names are found thereon, with their descendants thereafter born to them, with such persons as may intermarry according to tribal laws, shall alone constitute the several tribes which they represent."

By the act of 1896 applications for citizenship were required to be made to the commission within three months after the passage of that act, and to be passed upon by the commission within ninety days after made. Provision was also made for applications to the court or committee of the several tribes which were to be presented within three months and passed upon within thirty days. After the expiration of six months the commission was to make rolls of citizenship, adding the names of citizens whose right might be conferred under that act. After the expiration of the time fixed no new application for citizenship could be received, and the action of the commission upon those made within the time fixed was final, in the absence of an appeal to tne court. The act of 1897 did not provide for new applications for citizenship. It defined the words "rolls of citizenship," used in the act of 1896, and directed that all names appearing upon the rolls not coming within that definition should be open to investigation by the commission for a period of six months after the passage of said act. Neither did the act of 1898 make any provision for new applications for citizenship. The commission was authorized and directed to enroll the persons indicated and to investigate the right of all other persons whose names are found upon any tribal roll, and to omit all such as may have been placed there by fraud or without authority of law. They were not authorized to add any name not found upon some roll of the tribe, except those of descendants of persons rightfully upon some roll and persons intermarried with members of the tribes and therefore lawfully entitled to enrollment.

I wish in this discussion to draw clearly this distinction: The jurisdiction which the Government of the United States is seeking to exercise at this time is not to admit persons to citizenship. There is a distinction, and I hope I will be able to make myself clear on that point; there is a distinction, and a radical distinction, between admission to citizenship and the making up of tribal rolls. In 1896 Congress saw fit to take from the tribes the power to admit to citizenship, and as a result of that determination by Congress the act of June 10, 1896, was passed. That act provided that the tribal rolls, as then existing, should be confirmed, and that the Commission, as the representatives of the Government of the United States, should for three months have power to receive applications of persons who wished to be added to those rolls or admitted to citizenship. Under the provisions of the law of 1896, and under the provisions of that law only, has there ever been conferred power upon any tribunal, by the Congress of the United States, to admit the citizenship.

Senator LONG. Persons not on the rolls?

Mr. CORNISH. Persons not on the rolls and not in the enjoyment of a tribal status. Mr. Van Devanter considers that question most comprehensively in his opinion, to which I have referred.

Senator McCUMBER. That is, they could not admit to citizenship, and he so declared.

Mr. CORNISH. And not place them on the tribal rolls; no, sir.

Senator McCUMBER. I can see the distinction.

Mr. CORNISH. But I shall show later on, after I have concluded my discussion of the law of 1896, that the limit of power to the Commission to enroll persons are the rolls themselves and admissions under the law of 1896. Those are the two sources, and the two sources alone, from which the Commission and the Secretary of the Interior may at this time draw the crude material from which a perfect roll may be made. I say the only power which Congress has ever conferred upon any tribunal to fix in a person not upon a tribal roll and not in the enjoyment of the tribal status was contained in the act of June 10, 1896, and a consideration of that act has nothing to do with the consideration of these cases.

The committee will understand that it was under the act of June 10, 1896, that the applications of many thousands of persons were filed. They were passed on by the Commission, and an appeal was taken to the United States court, and those are the persons who are known as the "court claimants." Those persons had nothing to do with this class of persons. The persons who applied in 1896 were passed upon by the Commission. They were given the right to take an appeal to the United States court, or it was provided that the tribes might appeal, and the United States court passed finally on those cases. It was contended later by the tribes that fraud and perjury and wrongdoing had been done in the trial of those cases by the United States courts to such an extent that relief should be provided, and the Choctaw and Chickasaw citizenship court was created. Thus the entire class of persons arising under the act of 1896 was disposed of.

I now repeat the statement that there has never been and that there is not now any power vested in any tribunal of the Government of the United States to admit to citizenship except that power conferred upon the Commission to the Five Civilized Tribes and the United States court under the provisions of the act of June 10, 1896.

That which the Government of the United States has sought to do since 1898 has not been to fix the status of any person but to make over the tribal rolls, and to take as a basis the crude material which had been furnished the Commission and the courts in 1896 and by the tribes in their tribal rolls. The status of such persons as were admitted under that law of 1896 was just the same as if they had been put on the tribal rolls. After the law of 1896 was passed Congress said to the Commission "You shall make up the tribal rolls, and in doing that you shall look to two sources, and to two sources only, the tribal rolls and admissions to citizenship under the law of 1896." Now, under this law of 1898 the Commission proceeded to do that.

Mr. BALLINGER. Will you please read that provision of the law?

Mr. CORNISH. I will make myself clear as to that, Mr. Ballinger.

The CHAIRMAN. Was not that the law that also refers to the treaties?

Mr. CORNISH. Yes, sir; the law of 1898. Now, when the Commission proceeded to do that thing, to wit, to make up the rolls from those two sources, a question arose, as I stated, as to a proper construction of that law, for the purpose of fixing the Commission's jurisdiction. It was upon the law of 1898 and the question of the Commission's jurisdiction thereunder that the decision to which I have referred the committee was rendered.

Now after that decision was rendered those persons who were interested were still not willing to accept the law as declared by Mr. Van Devanter, and then it was that Congress was asked in the year 1900—two years after the passage of this law—to construe that law of 1898 and say what it meant. That is found in the act of May 31, 1900.

Mr. Ballinger. I do not want to interfere, but won't you please read the act of 1896?

Mr. Cornish. I do not think that is a proper requirement at this time.

The Chairman. I think, Mr. Ballinger, unless you desire to call attention to some manifest misstatement of Mr. Cornish, you should permit him to proceed without interruption.

Mr. Cornish. A manifest misstatement I do not object to, but I do not believe it is quite fair to ask that my argument be directed along the lines suggested by the opposing counsel.

Now, as I say, the law of 1898 was passed and the Commission proceeded under its construction of that law and the question arose as to its power and jurisdiction. The question of law was submitted to Mr. Van Devanter, and he rendered a most comprehensive opinion, declaring what the Commission's jurisdiction was, and still those applicants bombarded the Commission from Texas and Arkansas and various other States, and then it was that the law of 1898 was defined, or construed, and the construction contained in the act of May 31, 1900, is merely a reflection of the construction placed by Mr. Van Devanter on the law of 1898.

The act of May 31, 1900, is as follows:

That said Commission shall continue to exercise all authority heretofore conferred on it by law. But it shall not receive, consider, or make any record of any application of any person for enrollment as a member of any tribe in Indian Territory who has not been a recognized citizen thereof, and duly and lawfully enrolled or admitted as such, and its refusal of such applications shall be final when approved by the Secretary of the Interior; *Provided*, That any Mississippi Choctaw, duly identified as such by the United States Commission to the Five Civilized Tribes, shall have the right, at any time, prior to the approval of the final rolls of the Choctaws and Chickasaws by the Secretary of the Interior, to make settlement within the Choctaw-Chickasaw country, and on proof of the fact of bona fide settlement may be enrolled by the said United States Commission and by the Secretary of the Interior as Choctaws entitled to allotment; *Provided further*, That all contracts or agreements looking to the sale or incumbrance in any way of the lands to be allotted to said Mississippi Choctaws shall be null and void.

I do not see how the position of Congress could be made stronger or stated in plainer terms. The law of 1898 was passed, the Commission properly construed the law, and was proceeding in accordance with that proper construction, and refused to consider the applications of persons unless they could show one of two things, either that their names were upon some one of the tribal rolls, or that they had been admitted by the Commission or the courts in the exercise of their jurisdiction under the law of 1896.

Then the law was submitted to the Assistant Attorney-General for the Department of the Interior, and he rendered an opinion affirming the construction placed on that law by the Commission. Then they were still unwilling to accept it, and the matter was presented to Congress and this law was passed.

Senator Clark, of Wyoming. Judge Van Devanter rendered this opinion. Now, by what process were those people that you are speaking of still trying to get on the rolls?

Mr. Cornish. Which people?

Senator Clark, of Wyoming. The same ones who are represented here now. I would like you to state it right now, if you please. You say they were still being bombarded with applications.

Mr. Cornish. I did not mean Mr. Ballinger's people.

Senator CLARK, of Wyoming Well anybody—people who were not on the rolls were bombarding to be put on the rolls notwithstanding Judge Van Devanter's opinion Now, to whom did they apply?

Mr CORNISH To the Commission

Senator CLARK of Wyoming The Commission which rejected them? If the Commissioners were rejecting them, did they then have any appeal?

Mr CORNISH Yes, sir, to the Secretary of the Interior

Senator CLARK, of Wyoming But the Secretary of the Interior had already, through his Assistant Attorney-General, rendered this opinion which precluded them

Mr CORNISH Yes, sir

Senator CLARK, of Wyoming They did not come to Congress to have this interpretation passed You come to Congress to have that passed, so as to stop these continued applications

Mr CORNISH I do not say that we did We were representing the tribes at the time, and I think the suggestion as to the law was made by the Department

Senator CLARK, of Wyoming I do not mean you personally, but the tribes were seeking to have these applications stopped

Mr CORNISH It was stopped by the Secretary of the Interior and Mr Van Devanter

Senator CLARK, of Wyoming I understand, but without that opinion, or without that declaration of Congress, there was no way under the ruling of the Department of the Interior that they could be added to the rule anyway

Mr CORNISH No, sir

Senator CLARK, of Wyoming So that that was simply a declaration of the policy of the Department at that time

Mr CORNISH Yes, sir, that was the proper construction of the original law that was passed

Mr McMURRAY I desire to say that it has been suggested that we are here asking for this law I wanted to suggest that those people are here insisting that this law be liberalized and broadened, and this was the conclusion that was reached by the committee

Senator CLARK, of Wyoming I had supposed that this was simply a declaration that would relieve the Secretary of the Interior from—

Mr CORNISH Congress took the responsibility

Now, I have anticipated somewhat Senator Clark asked me how those people were bombarding the Commission to the Five Civilized Tribes and the Secretary of the Interior, petitioning to have their claims passed on upon their merits I did not have reference to the people who are represented by Mr Ballinger They were never heard of as applicants until less than two years ago

I shall briefly give the committee a history of how this matter arose This proposition was given birth by Mr Campbell, present law officer for the Interior Department. A great many persons have agreed with his view since that time, but he is the pioneer of this proposition, and upon the rendition by him, some two years ago, of this very remarkable opinion, the inspiration was given these people, after their enrollment for a lifetime as freedmen, that they might be enrolled as Indians. I did not have reference, in giving early history of citizenship matters, to these people at all; I had reference to these people who came in ox wagons and various other ways from the various other States when they heard that the Indian land was to be divided up. A great many people came from the State of Arkansas and the State of Texas, and from other surrounding States, conceiving that they probably had rights. We have all heard the term "an Indian right." There were 50,000 persons—nearly double the present citizenship population of the Choctaw and Chickasaw Nation, who claimed that they had "a right," and were sufficiently interested to move into the Indian country and make application.

Senator LONG. And if they did, it was the best business venture they could make.

Mr. CORNISH. Yes, sir. There are 50,000 of them in all who have bombarded the Commission from 1898 to the present time, and it has taken all the wisdom and ingenuity of the Government of the United States and its representatives to prevent the property of the tribes from being absolutely taken away by this horde of adventurers. The records show many instances of perjury and wrongdoing, and everything that should be condemned by men who think rightly.

Those are the persons I had reference to. The Commission said, "You are not on a tribal roll; you have not been admitted by the Commission in pursuance of the jurisdiction given in the act of 1898, and there is no power for us to consider your application on its merits." Mr. Van Devanter passed upon the matter, as did also Congress in the law which I have just read.

Now, I shall refer to the persons represented by Mr. Ballinger. They had nothing to do with these proceedings. They have grown up in very recent times. The committee will understand that under the treaty of 1866, was to the Choctaws and Chickasaws what the reconstruction acts were to the other Southern communities. The treaty of 1866 was the treaty by which the relations of the tribes with the Government of the United States were reestablished. The Choctaws and Chickasaws joined with the Southern Confederacy, and after the war the treaty of 1866 was made for the purpose of reestablishing the tribal relations of those Indians with the Government of the United States. That treaty provided that the Choctaws and Chickasaws might within two years adopt their slaves—their freedmen (slaves known since technically as freedmen)—and confer upon them the right to have, in the event of tribal allotments later on, allotments to the amount of 40 acres each, and that if they failed to do that they were to forfeit their interest in a certain fund of $300,000, which arose from the lease of certain western lands.

The Choctaws saw fit to pass an act of adoption, conferring this right on Choctaw freedmen, and a roll of Choctaw freedmen was made which has been followed by the Government of the United States in making up the final rolls of the Choctaw freedmen. The Chickasaws did not see fit to do that; they preferred to forfeit their interests in $300,000 to conferring these property rights upon the freedmen. From 1866 to 1898 the matter of the status of the Chickasaw freedmen stood, in so far as fixing their status as freedmen was concerned, unadjusted and undetermined, and then it was that the Choctaws and Chickasaws, who had never been accused of lack of consideration and generosity either to their own people or to any people to whom they were under obligation, acting upon the request and upon the insistence of the representatives of the Government of the United States when the treaty of 1898 was made, agreed to include a provision for the allotment of 40 acres each to Chickasaw freedmen

Senator LONG What section?

Mr CORNISH It is contained in section 29

Senator McCUMBER Of the law of 1898

Mr CORNISH Yes, sir, in what is known as the Atoka agreement—

That the Commission to the Five Civilized Tribes shall make a correct roll of Chickasaw freedmen

Now, the committee will understand that no roll of Chickasaw freedmen had been made up to that time the Choctaws had, but the Chickasaws had not adopted their freedmen until this time, so they provided that they should make a correct roll of Chickasaw freedmen entitled to any rights or benefits under the treaty made in 1866 between the United States and the Choctaw and the Chickasaw tribes and their descendants born to them since the date of said treaty

That is only for making the roll Here is what they agreed

And forty acres of land, including their present residences and improvements, shall be allotted to each, to be selected, held, and used by them until their rights under said treaty shall be determined in such manner as shall hereafter be provided by act of Congress

That was not an ungenerous act on the part of the Choctaws and Chickasaws They felt, as a matter of law, that they had the privilege given them under the treaty of 1866 to adopt these freedmen and give them the 40 acres of land or the forfeit of $300,000 They felt, for reasons evidently sufficient to them, that the better proposition would be to forfeit their interest in the $300,000 and not adopt the freedmen, but understand, gentlemen, that the freedmen were not expelled from the Choctaw and Chickasaw nations the Chickasaw freedmen had enjoyed all rights of freedmen citizenship, they had occupied lands without question and they have been permitted to participate in the land, the benefits of the property of the Choctaws and Chickasaws from 1866 down to 1898 in all respects as though they had been adopted under the provisions of the treaty of 1866

So when you came to make the treaty of 1898 the Indians were willing to listen to you, and they settled that question so far as the negroes were concerned, they provided that they should be enrolled and given 40-acre allotments to be held until such time as Congress should make provision for a judicial determination of the question of their adoption

Now, when the treaty of 1902 was made, the freedmen had been enrolled, they had gone into possession of the land, they had had their rights fixed, but there was a controversy between the Chickasaws and the Government of the United States as to whether or not those lands legally belonged to the Chickasaw freedmen, and in the treaty of 1902 a provision was inserted that the question of law should be referred to the Court of Claims for determination of the question of law as to whether or not those freedmen were or were not under the treaty of 1866 entitled to the land We presented the suit to the Court of Claims and our views were sustained by that court and judgment was rendered against the Government of the United States for the value of those lands The money has not been paid as yet, but the decree of the court has been rendered and it only remains to determine how many freedmen there are, in order that it may be determined what sum of money the Government of the United States shall pay to the Chickasaws.

Senator LONG. Was that case appealed?

Mr. CORNISH. Yes, sir; it was appealed to the Supreme Court of the United States and affirmed.

Now, gentlemen, that is the history of the Chickasaw freedmen, as an abstract proposition. I shall now apply it to these persons.

The Commission proceeded under the law in the fall of 1898 to make up the rolls of Choctaw and Chickasaw citizens and Choctaw and Chickasaw freedmen. The first meeting was held at Stonewall in the Chickasaw Nation; the next at Pauls Valley; the next at Ardmore; the next at Tishomingo; the next at Lebanon; the next at Colbert; the next at Duncan, and the next at Chickasha. A wagon trip was made through that country, the Commission camping for a considerable time at each appointment. The Choctaw and Chickasaw Indians applied to the Commission to be enrolled as Choctaw and Chickasaw citizens. Choctaw and Chickasaw freedmen voluntarily applied before that Commission at that time, and every man, woman, and child residing in that country and represented by Mr. Ballinger, at that time voluntarily applied to the Commission to be enrolled as Chickasaw freedmen, and were accordingly enrolled in order that the rights which were given them by this treaty of 1898 in the 40 acres of land might be fixed.

It has been suggested that some affidavits have been filed tending to show that these people claimed at that time that they were Chickasaw Indians. There are statements in the record made up by the select committee in the Indian Territory in which all the circumstances under which those applications were taken are set out by Mr. Bixby, who is personally known to you gentlemen, and who has been actually chairman of that Commission for more than six years, who has been its practical head since the year 1897, in which he states that it was not suggested by a single man, woman, or child in this class, or a single man, woman, or child who applied as a Chickasaw freedman to have their rights established as Chickasaw freedmen, that they were entitled to their rights as Choctaw and Chickasaw Indians. That evidence is corroborated by Captain McKennon. I do not know how many of you gentlemen are acquainted with Capt. A. S. McKennon, who had particular charge of this work. Mr. Bixby's evidence is in the record. He had charge of that part of the Commission's work which had to do with the enrollment of Indians, and Captain McKennon and his corps of assistants had to do with that part of the work which related to the enrollment of freedmen.

They conferred frequently and their testimony is absolutely and positively to the effect that this proposition was not heard of at that time, and never until the rendition of this remarkable opinion of Mr. Campbell's. The statement that there were persons swarming around the Commission and forced to go to the freedmen's tent— that statement is absolutely untrue. I accuse no one of willful misrepresentation, but I do say, in the light of the facts as shown by the record, that the statement is absolutely and unqualifiedly false.

Senator McCUMBER. May it not be true that many of the freedmen in attempting to ascertain where they should go to be enrolled might probably have gone to the wrong place, and have been directed to go to the other, and that many of those who were entitled to be enrolled as members of the tribe might have gone to the wrong place and have been directed to the right place?

Mr. CORNISH. Mr. Bixby and Captain McKennon say not. Their testimony covers that point conclusively.

Senator McCUMBER. It would be strange if they did not.

Mr. CORNISH. Of course, some might have gotten into the wrong tent.

Senator CLARK, of Wyoming. I have an indistinct recollection of something on that point coming out in the testimony. The two classes of Indians, by blood, and the freedmen, did they have at each of those places representatives to direct their people?

Mr. CORNISH. Yes, sir.

Senator CLARK, of Wyoming. I have an indistinct recollection of something of that sort—that the evidence was that they were misdirected.

Mr. CORNISH. I am perfectly willing, if this committee has authority to administer oaths, to make a sworn statement with regard to that.

The CHAIRMAN. Of course the committee has the power to administer oaths.

Mr. CORNISH. I wish to make a statement myself. I want the committee to understand that that is not the fact. As I understand, you want definite information on that point at this time. I was an employee of the Commission to the Five Civilized Tribes myself at this time, and——

The CHAIRMAN. To save any question, Senator Clark, I do not think there is any question whatever that the committee can administer oaths.

Senator CLARK, of Wyoming. Certainly not.

Senator McCUMBER. We can get along just as well with it as without it.

The CHAIRMAN. I understand that you are a member of the bar, Mr. Cornish.

Mr. CORNISH. Yes, sir. I went with the Commission in September, 1898, as one of its employees. I am a stenographer, and was a stenographer before I began to practice law, and I was the clerk or the assistant to Captain McKennon. I took these applications myself. In fact, I took every application—that is, I sat as Captain McKennon's clerk. He was the Commissioner and I was his clerk to take down such data as he dictated and such things as he directed with reference to applications of Chickasaw freedmen. I was present at the making of every individual application in the Chickasaw Nation, and I have a personal knowledge——

Senator CLARK, of Wyoming. Of the freedmen?

Mr. CORNISH. Yes, sir: I was in that department, and I have a personal knowledge of everything that transpired from the first day of the Commission's appointment at Stonewall to the last day of the Commission's appointment at Chickasaw—a period of two and a half months—and I say here, as I said to the Commission in Indian Territory, that I was present when these applications were presented, and every application of every Chickasaw freedman was voluntary upon his part, and there was not a word or a suggestion coming from any single individual Chickasaw freedman applicant, or anyone representing those applicants, to show that there was any doubt in the minds of those people as to what their rights were, or any controversy either in their minds or the minds of anyone else, as to whether they were entitled to enrollment as Indians. They had applied as freedmen, as they had always been, and were so enrolled.

Senator BRANDEGEE. Were you in the tent where the applicants for enrollment by blood applied?

Mr. CORNISH. Occasionally I was; I was the only stenographer with the Commission at the time, and when any question of fact arose in the tent where they were enrolling Indians they would send for me to come over and report the testimony in a particular case of the application of an Indian; but to that extent only was I in that tent.

Senator BRANDEGEE. Would you know if a freedman applied to be enrolled as an Indian by blood in a tent where they were enrolling Indians by blood, and whether he was directed to go to the other tent or not?

Mr. CORNISH. I do not say that; I am simply speaking about matters as far as I know. I said the fact of my participation——

Senator BRANDEGEE. I understood you to say that you were familiar with every single applicant?

Mr. CORNISH. As to the enrollment of freedmen.

Senator BRANDEGEE. I am assuming that a freedman applies in the Indian-by-blood tent for enrollment—you can not state whether he was put out of that tent and directed to the other or not.

Mr. CORNISH. I do not attempt to state that. I do state the matters which I know of personally. I know everything that transpired in the freedmen tent; I was present when everything was done in that tent and with regard to that branch of the work, and I was only in the other tent at stated times. Of course whatever transpired when I was in the other tent I have no personal knowledge of; but I know personally of everything that transpired in the freedmen tent with reference to these particular applicants, and I do know that it was not suggested by any of these people that they had rights as Indians.

Senator LA FOLLETTE. If there had been any controversies with regard to the matter it would have occurred in the other tent, would it not? That is where the struggle would take place.

Mr. CORNISH. Yes, sir.

Senator LA FOLLETTE. And if they were sent out of that tent and told that they could not register there and the other tent was the only place where they could get registration, they would be likely to go over there quietly and take what they could get?

Mr. CORNISH. Of course, I do not presume to state of my own personal knowledge what transpired in the Indian tent. I will state with regard to the statement that I now make that this proposition is confirmed by the testimony of Mr. Bixby, who was in charge of the work of enrolling Indians, and the testimony of Mr. Hopkins, who was the chief clerk of that tent.

Senator BRANDEGEE. There is an affidavit on file by some gentleman, whose name I do not now remember, who was also an employee of the Commission. He was in the tent where the Indians for enrollment by blood applied, and he makes some statements there which you have pronounced to be false. His statement was upon his own knowledge. Your statement of what took place in that tent and what did not is of a negative character, and I wanted to know if it was your intention to brand that statement of his as a falsehood here and now

Mr Cornish Of course, I do not know what that statement is

Mr Ballinger Mr Chairman, may I ask Mr Cornish one question?

The Chairman Yes

Mr Ballinger Is your name W A Smiley?

Mr Cornish My name? No, sir

Mr Ballinger He was the stenographer who took much of this testimony running all the way through it

Mr Cornish What is the date of the paper that you hold in your hand?

Mr Ballinger April 18, 1899

Mr Cornish This was in 1898 You are a year off

Mr Ballinger This was all taken under the same act, was it not?

Mr Cornish These proceedings to which I refer were in the months of September, October and November of 1898

Mr Ballinger These people were examined under the act of 1898, were they not?

Mr Cornish Yes but that is not a matter for me to discuss I am perfectly willing that the committee shall understand the facts which I state but the time when these applications were taken was in the fall of 1898

Senator McCumber Were any others taken at any other time to determine the status of these people?

Mr Cornish Any applications?

Senator McCumber Yes

Mr Cornish The Commission made another tour through the Choctaw Nation in 1899, but most of these applications were taken in 1898

Senator Clark, of Wyoming As to those, you have nothing to say?

Mr Cornish No, sir I was not with them then

Senator Sutherland As I understand you, all you claim in your statement as to the facts is that you were in this freedmen tent, and that so far as appearances there were concerned there was no indication that they were making any claim to be enrolled as freedmen under any sort of duress, and that as to what happened in the other tent before you went there you do not know anything about?

Mr Cornish No, sir, I do state that my evidence on that point is corroborated by Mr McKennon and Mr Bixby

Senator Long That evidence is all in here

Mr Cornish Yes, sir, it is part of the evidence you have of the select committee

Senator Stone And they testified that no such thing occurred?

Mr Cornish Yes, sir

Senator McCumber Let me ask you one question If so important a subject as a claim of right on the part of these freedmen to be enrolled as citizens of the tribe had been known or discussed at that time, would you have known it?

Mr Cornish I think I would certainly have known it

Senator McCumber Well, was there anything of that kind, or did you hear any discussion of that character at all?

Mr Cornish I have stated that I have no information or knowledge of it in any way

Senator McCumber. In either of the tents?

Mr. Cornish. No, sir; I was familiar in a general way with the progress of the work of the Commission, because after the applications of the day were over we would meet at night and work until very late, and we were all familiar in a general way with what had transpired in other branches of the Commission's work, but I have absolutely no knowledge of any such claim having been made by any one of those people.

Senator Sutherland. Let me ask you a question; I have not been here all the time, and it may have been covered before. There are some affidavits here from persons who claim that they were denied the right to be enrolled as citizens.

Mr. Cornish. I do not understand so; I have not seen them.

Senator McCumber. Those affidavits, I understand, were made the succeeding year.

Senator Sutherland. There are some that were made in 1898. Now, did you examine those affidavits?

Mr. Cornish. No, sir; I have not seen them.

Senator Sutherland. Has anybody at any time attempted to meet the statements in those affidavits?

Mr. Cornish. No, sir; I was coming to that.

Senator Dubois. I do not know what is stated in those affidavits, as I have not read them over, but did any freedmen, in accepting his enrollment as a freedman, protest at the same time that he was entitled to enrollment as a citizen?

Mr. Cornish. As to that I should have a personal knowledge, because I was there. No, sir; they did not, not in a single instance as I recall, and I think I would recall it if there had been such an instance. With regard to that matter I have a personal knowledge.

Senator Dubois. I do not know whether these affidavits cover that or not.

Senator Sutherland. If they had been directed in those other tents to come to the freedmen tent, and had been told there that they could not be enrolled as citizens would they have been likely to have made a protest?

Mr. Cornish. I think not likely. I want to be perfectly fair about this matter. I think really if a controversy had arisen in the other tent, and thrashed out there, and the freedmen had been forced to come to the freedmen tent, I do not think any controversy would have arisen in the freedmen tent, but in a general way if that had arisen I would have known of it.

Senator Sutherland. Who were present in the other tent where they were being enrolled as citizens?

Mr. Cornish. Mr. Bixby and Colonel Needles, of Illinois.

Senator Sutherland. They were both there all the time?

Mr. Cornish. Yes, sir; they had some three or four clerks. Colonel Needles was not present when the evidence was taken at Muscogee.

Senator Sutherland. Mr. Bixby was there all the time, was he?

Mr. Cornish. Yes, sir.

Senator Sutherland. Now, do both of those gentlemen make statements in conflict with these affidavits?

Mr. Cornish. Colonel Needles does not make any statement at all. He is not a member of the Commission.

Senator Sutherland. He was then. Was any attempt made to get a statement from him? He is still living, is he not?

Mr Cornish Yes, sir the testimony of Mr Bixby and Captain McKennon and the testimony of Mr Hopkins and my testimony (I was clerk to Captain McKennon) was taken There is no conflict in that evidence I understand that these affidavits tend to contradict that evidence That evidence was taken before the Commission in the Indian Territory, and there was nothing tending to contradict that evidence, and I do not think it would be quite reasonable and fair to reach a conclusion of fact now, if that particular fact is of importance, and I presume it is of some importance I do not believe it would be quite fair that that conclusion of fact should be resolved in favor of these affidavits which have been put in as against a solemn oral evidence of the officials of the Government of the United States, whose officers must be presumed to have done their duty In the absence of a clear showing to the contrary, it must be so presumed They are able and distinguished men and good men, so far as anybody knows, and I do not believe that their solemn statements, they being representatives of the Government of the United States, and having been presumed to have done their duty, and having testified positively and unequivocally as to these facts should be rejected I do not believe the issue of fact should be resolved against their evidence and in favor of these affidavits, taken here and there, all over the country, and put in here

Senator Stone Did your Commissioner, Captain McKennon, send Indians over to the other tent?

Mr Cornish Not to my knowledge There is this fact that must be taken into consideration That matter was superintended in a way by a commission of some six or seven members, who represented the Indians and who saw to their enrollment and assisted them It was a commission composed of the leading men of the Choctaw and Chickasaw nations, who sat with Mr Bixby in the enrollment of the Indians, not only that but at the suggestion of the Commission itself, a commission of freedmen was created for the purpose of sitting with Captain McKennon in the enrollment of those freedmen

Senator Brandegee In view of your remark and as I have read all this testimony, and these affidavits and whether it reflects on anybody or not, or what the fact is I do not know there are affidavits there, and there is one affidavit in particular, by the very gentleman who you are now speaking of, and who you say is a good man, who represented the Choctaw or Chickasaw freedmen, who states just what was done, and he complains that he was ordered to make all of his people go to the freedmen tent if they had any negro blood in them at all and they were inclined to be enrolled as Indians

Mr Cornish That he states in a general way at least, I presume he does But the tent presided over by Captain McKennon was for the enrollment of freedmen and the tent presided over by Mr Bixby was for the enrollment of Indians

Senator Brandegee No, he states in a very clear way that they were compelled to go to the other tent in spite of their claims that they were entitled to be enrolled as Indians

Mr Cornish When the select committee was at Ardmore this man, Charles Cohee, was there I saw him and we talked of what occurred at that time, and when at Ardmore I presumed that this man would be brought before your committee, he was there I had a conversation with him with a view to ascertaining what his evidence would be and whether or not he would make a statement which would conflict with this other evidence, and he did not so state to me. I rehearsed with him the facts which occurred at that time, and asked him as to those various incidents, and he did not make any statement to me of a contrary nature.

Senator BRANDEGEE. Had you these affidavits at that time?

Mr. CORNISH. I had not.

Senator BRANDEGEE. At what date were we at Ardmore?

Mr. CORNISH. I think about the 18th, 19th, or 20th of November, 1906.

Mr. BALLINGER. This affidavit was made on the 28th day of November, 1905.

Mr. CORNISH. This man was at Ardmore. I had heard rumors to the effect that there were various persons who had ideas as to what occurred in 1898, and I saw this man at Ardmore and renewed my acquaintance with him and expected that he would be brought before the committee. He made no statement to me of any knowledge as to any facts that would contradict the facts as I understand them, as well as Mr. Bixby and Mr. Hopkins. He was there, but was not brought before the committee.

Mr. BRANDEGEE. Are you willing to read his affidavit now?

Mr. CORNISH. I have no objection to doing so.

Mr. BRANDEGEE. I would like to hear it because it brings out the points in controversy.

Mr. CORNISH. The affidavit is as follows:

AFFIDAVIT OF CHARLES COHEE.

UNITED STATES OF AMERICA,
   Indian Territory, Southern Judicial District:

CHARLES COHEE, first being duly sworn, on oath states that he is 57 years of age; resident of the Chickasaw Nation, Indian Territory, and lives at the town of Berwyn, in said nation and Territory; that he is enrolled as a Chickasaw freedman, and that on the 1st day of September, 1898, he was appointed by R. N. Harris, governor of the Chickasaw Nation, a member of the committee to sit with the Dawes Commission for the purpose of identifying applicants for enrollment as freedmen; that he was again appointed to the same position by Governor Johnson in April, 1899, and that he worked every day with the Commission during their sittings in the Chickasaw Nation, and most of the time during their sittings in the Choctaw Nation.

Affiant further states that at the beginning of the work the committee of which he was a member in making statements to the Dawes Commission of the status of applicants made particular mention of those who claimed to have Indian blood; that the applications of such persons claiming Indian blood were for awhile received by the Commission, but that in a short time, about fifteen days after the committee began its sittings, all such applications were rejected by the said Dawes Commission, and the committee of which affiant was a member was informed that these applicants who were born to slave mothers or to negro women who were descendants of slaves, were freedmen, and would be enrolled as such only, and the said committee was advised to discontinue hearing the statement of applicants as to their Indian blood, as in no case would they be enrolled as Indian citizens; and that therefore the said committee from that time on, with possibly a few exceptions, refused to hear statements of persons of mixed colored blood, of their claim that they were possessed of Indian blood in any degree whatever; that the said committee from that time on, in stating to the Commission status of applicants, only made mention of such family relations as would establish their rights as freedmen, and made no mention whatever of the existence of Indian blood, although in many instances they know applicants were possessed of such.

                                                                    CHARLES COHEE.

Subscribed and sworn to before me this 21st day of November, 1905.

[SEAL.]   J. A. McNAUGHT,
                                                            Notary Public.

My commission expires March 17, 1900.

That statement is not true This committee was selected by the freedmen Out of the generosity of the Chickasaws this commission of freedmen, sitting with the Commission for the purpose of enrolling the freedmen, was paid by the Chickasaws out of the treasury of the nation but this committee was selected by a meeting of negroes for that purpose

Senator CLARK, of Wyoming Somebody certainly supervised that selection

Mr CORNISH They had a convention of Chickasaw freedman, or an organization, and that association or organization picked out this committee Now, when the matter of the pay of the Indian enrollments came up it was suggested by the Commission that the Chickasaws should pay this commission, and that was done by warrants on the treasury

Senator LA FOLLETTE As a foundation for that, is it not possible that a selection may have been made following the selection of the freedmen?

Mr CORNISH Of course it is possible, but I am sure such was not the case

Senator LA FOLLETTE Your general knowledge and special acquaintance would not preclude the possibility of then having made some appointment which you did not know about?

Mr CORNISH Governor Johnston approved the act which appropriated money for this purpose

Senator STONE Do you know anything about that affidavit?

Mr CORNISH No sir

Senator STONE Do you know who prepared it?

Mr CORNISH I do not

Mr ALBERT J LEE I will say that I myself prepared it at my office in Ardmore, Ind T

Senator McCUMBER It is stated that for the first fifteen days they did admit the freedmen to citizenship What do you know about that?

Mr CORNISH I know that nothing of that kind transpired to my knowledge, and Mr Bixby states the same I know also that this man Cohee was constantly in the freedmen tent for the first fifteen days and for the whole time

Senator McCUMBER When was this separate tent for the freedmen established?

Mr CORNISH It was three days before the Commission began to sit

Senator McCUMBER Before anything was done?

Mr CORNISH Yes, sir I desire to say that it is not my purpose to reflect on anybody, but I do mean to suggest this, with all the earnestness I can command, that if there is a question of fact in this proposition, and that fact may influence your disposition of this particular proposition, I do not believe it is quite fair and reasonable to disregard the positive evidence of Captain McKennon, Mr Bixby, and the various other official subordinates upon this proposition and overturn the facts which that evidence establishes, or tends to establish, upon these affidavits taken and offered in this way, when positive evidence could have been offered contradicting that orally before the select committee when in the Indian Territory

Senator McCUMBER The important matter, it seems to me, is whether they are entitled under the laws and treaties

Mr CORNISH Exactly, but these alleged facts are urged for the purpose of discrediting the Commission

Senator BRANDEGEE But if they were entitled, and entitled under the treaty, under a certain construction of that word "descendants," and were ignorant of it, and the Commission has prevented their being enrolled, would that have any bearing on the matter, in your judgment?

Mr CORNISH It might have a bearing upon Congress in providing that exact justice be done, if, as a result of that, injustice had been done

The CHAIRMAN The committee will now take a recess until 1 30 o'clock

AFTER RECESS

Mr CORNISH Mr Chairman and gentlemen of the committee, we were considering a procedure adopted by the Commission under the law of 1898, to do the field work necessary to make up the tribal rolls The statement was made on yesterday, evidently for the purpose of prejudicing the Commission in the minds of this committee, that the Commission has not done its duty in the matter of these applications and making up these records

Now, as bearing on that proposition, the statement is made by Mr Ballinger that the law itself required that the evidence of these people be taken down in a certain way, and that that was not done That statement was evidently made for the purpose of putting the Commission in a bad light before this committee, as, according to his contention, that would be one of the reasons why relief should be given in this particular class of cases Now, when the law is examined it appears that that statement is not correct That is one of his flagrantly incorrect statements

Mr BALLINGER Mr Chairman---

Mr CORNISH I shall do you perfect justice, Mr Ballinger

The CHAIRMAN Mr Ballinger, unless you desire to call the speaker's attention to something that you think he is seriously mistaken about, I suggest that he be allowed to proceed without interruption

Senator CLARK, of Wyoming My impression was that Mr Ballinger rose to question Mr Cornish's statement of his position

Mr BALLINGER I will state the purpose for which I arose I was asked by Senator Brandegee whether the instructions were contained in the statute, or were contained in the departmental instructions, and I stated specifically that they were contained in departmental instructions

Mr CORNISH The direct statement was made that the requirement was contained in the face of the law, that this evidence was to be taken, and the procedure taken in a certain way

Now, I call the committee's attention to that part of the law, which does not contain any such statement It says that the Commission shall be authorized and directed to make correct rolls of the citizens by blood of all the other tribes, etc

And in another part of this same law—this is the only provision defining how the Commission shall proceed—and it says

Said Commission shall make such rolls descriptive of the persons thereon, so that they may be thereby identified and it is authorized to take a census of each of said tribes or to adopt any other means by them deemed necessary to enable them to make such rolls

Now, under this provision of that law, it appears that the statement that the proceedings of the Commission should be conducted in any particular way is incorrect. Then Mr Ballinger made the statement as to how their proceedings should be conducted, that it was contained in departmental instructions. Now I would like to see those instructions

Senator BRANDEGEE. While Mr Ballinger is looking for that paper I would like to ask you a question

Mr CORNISH. I will be very glad to furnish any information that may be desired

Senator BRANDEGEE. I wanted to ask you this. If it should be determined that the word "descendants" as used in the treaty of 1830, meant physical issue, to use your language, then could Congress constitutionally pass an act which would deprive those people of their right to enrollment?

Mr CORNISH. Well, yes I think the exercise of that power would be sustained----

Senator BRANDEGEE. I did not want to suggest that you be heard on that point, but it occurred to me that it was a material point

Mr CORNISH. I think the exercise of such power would be sustained

Senator BRANDEGEE. My point is, if the treaty fixes the list of persons, can Congress alter it?

Mr CORNISH. That is the question you raised this morning. We have always contended that the treaty should govern, that a mere act of Congress would not set aside a treaty provision, but there are many who take the opposite view of that matter

Senator CLARK, of Wyoming. But your individual view is that if Mr Ballinger's definition of the word "descendants" is a correct view---

Mr CORNISH. I do not quite see how we would get at that, because I can not assume that it means what he says it means

Senator CLARK, of Wyoming. You can not assume, but you can assume for the purpose of answering my question, or giving me such light as you have, assuming - we will not say Mr Ballinger's view—but assuming that the view of Assistant Attorney-General Campbell is correct in that respect, how then would it be necessary---

Mr CORNISH. I think I get your idea. If it were written in the face of the treaty of 1830---

Senator CLARK, of Wyoming. You still do not get my idea

Mr CORNISH. I think I do

Senator CLARK, of Wyoming. I know you do not get the view that is in my mind

The CHAIRMAN. I suggest that you let Senator Clark have the privilege of stating his question

Mr CORNISH. Excuse me

Senator CLARK, of Wyoming. My understanding is that Attorney-General Campbell interprets the word "descendants" as it is used in the treaty—he interprets that to mean any person who has in his veins Indian blood, notwithstanding the fact that he may also have other blood. That, I understand, to be Attorney-General Campbell's interpretation of the word "descendants."

Mr. CORNISH. In effect.

Senator CLARK, of Wyoming. Now, accepting, for the sake of the hypothetical question, that his interpretation is correct, then how would you answer Senator Brandegee's question?

Mr. CORNISH. If his interpretation is correct, and that is what the treaty means, then his people would be entitled. That is true.

Senator WARNER. And Congress ought not to deprive them of it.

Mr. CORNISH. I may say that some very distinguished people differ on that proposition.

Senator CLARK, of Wyoming. And your opinion would be that Congress could not?

Mr. CORNISH. I do not know that I could intelligently define my view on that question. I have not considered it sufficiently.

Senator CLARK, of Wyoming. Suppose, instead of the word "descendants" it was "full-blood Choctaw Indians" in the treaty; could Congress pass a law cutting off the rights of the full-blood Choctaw Indians?

Mr. CORNISH. Of course you desire my view. There are many views on that subject.

Senator CLARK, of Wyoming. I want your view—not as binding on this case, or as especially influencing this particular case.

Mr. CORNISH. Well, in the light of the decision of the Circuit Court of Appeals. in a case which has recently been presented to it, and in the light of an opinion which, I think, the Supreme Court will render in a very short time on that question, I believe Congress has that power.

Senator CLARK, of Wyoming. You believe that Congress has the power? .

Mr. CORNISH. Yes, sir; in other words, I believe that the courts of this land would sustain that power if Congress saw fit to exercise it.

Senator CLARK, of Wyoming. Your view is that the present decisions and those that are looked for by the Supreme Court——

Mr. CORNISH. Yes, sir; would sustain that power, if exercised.

Senator CLARK, of Wyoming. You believe, then, under the present decisions of the court, and the decisions that are to be looked for, that the Supreme Court would say that Congress had the exclusive right to make those rolls upon its own motion, without reference to any tribal rights that may have theretofore been bestowed?

Mr. CORNISH. Yes, sir; I think the courts would sustain that power if Congress saw fit to exercise it. I have not considered it sufficiently to mature my own view definitely. Academically speaking, I do not know whether I believe that is the law or not, but I do believe the courts of the land would sustain the power if Congress saw fit to exercise it.

Senator WARNER. That is, if the treaty provided that only full-blood Choctaws should be enrolled, that Congress would have the power to say that only half breeds should be enrolled?

Mr. CORNISH. Yes, sir; I believe that.

Senator CLARK, of Wyoming. In other words, Congress has plenary power in the matter, you think?

Mr Cornish I am reflecting what the decisions of the courts would be, in my judgment

Senator Brandegee In the opinion of Mr Van Devanter, which you handed in this morning—without reading that particular decision—does he discuss the meaning of the word "descendants" in the treaty of 1830?

Mr Cornish No sir I do not think he does

Senator Brandegee. That was in the decision that was spoken of yesterday by Mr Ballinger?

Mr Cornish I understood that he referred to some decision of a court in Alabama

Senator Brandegee: That decision which Senator Clark alluded to a few moments ago by Mr Campbell, what case is referred to in that?

Senator Clark, of Wyoming It was the Perry case, where it was decided that if the person had Indian blood he was of necessity the the descendant of an Indian and entitled to enrollment

Senator Brandegee. How does that opinion of Mr Van Devanter, which you handed me this morning—if it does not discuss the meaning of the word "descendant" as used in the treaty of 1830—have any bearing on the present question?

Mr Cornish In this way, that the treaty of 1898, which the decision of Mr Van Devanter discusses, and the subsequent laws passed in pursuance of that treaty, provides that the commission to the Five Civilized Tribes, and various other tribunals of the Government of the United States shall, in the making up of the rolls of citizenship, be limited to persons whose names appear on the tribal roll, which tribal rolls were made in pursuance of the laws, customs, and usages of the tribes

Senator Brandegee But does it not also say that it shall be made with reference to the treaty rights?

Mr Cornish It says so in terms, and the subsequent law reflects the holding of Mr Van Devanter It is simply the legislative confirmation of a judicial opinion It says that no person shall be enrolled unless the name of that person appears on some roll of the tribe

Senator Brandegee: May I make this suggestion to you—and I do not want to tell you how you shall try your case, but having been through these papers which have been filed by Mr Ballinger, representing his side of the case—I notice that wherever he has referred to a statute bearing on this matter he has inserted the full statute, and I think we could get a more coherent idea of your claim when we read your statement if you would also insert the full statute instead of an excerpt

Mr Cornish I think the inference that I have omitted anything that bears on this controversy is somewhat unfair

Senator Brandegee I do not mean that any such inference shall be drawn, but I do mean that when I am called upon to construe a statute I would like to see the whole of it

Mr Cornish I have given such references to statutes so that they can readily be found, and in many instances I have quoted them

Senator Clark, of Wyoming I think you had better do as Senator Brandegee suggests, because there is a good deal of this matter that we will have to go over

Senator STONE. Before you proceed, Mr. Cornish, I would like to ask you, as a question of fact—which I suppose you can answer—when the treaty of 1830 was made, these Indians were all living there?

Mr. CORNISH. Yes, sir.

Senator STONE. Were they slave owners and holders at that time?

Mr. CORNISH. Yes, sir.

Senator STONE. Did they take their slaves with them to the Territory?

Mr. CORNISH. Yes, sir; they did, just as they did their cattle and other property.

Senator STONE. When they moved there?

Mr. CORNISH. Yes, sir.

Senator STONE. I asked those questions in order to ascertain the condition at the time the treaty was made.

Mr. CORNISH. There is no question that at the time they immigrated they took their slaves as well as their other property.

Senator WARNER. What do I understand your conclusions to be as to Mr. Van Devanter's decision?

Mr. CORNISH. My conclusion is that it is therein held that the Government of the United States in making up the tribal rolls—the rolls of those persons to participate in the distribution of the tribal property, shall be only those persons who have been enrolled by the tribes themselves in pursuance of their laws, customs, and usages. I understand that to be his holding, and that holding is reflected in the law of the next year.

Senator WARNER. And their descendants?

Mr. CORNISH. And their descendants born since the tribal rolls were made, and the tribal rolls to which I have reference were made in 1893 and 1896.

Now I call on Mr. Ballinger for the instructions to which he referred a few moments ago. You understand that the statement yesterday—and the statement which I contradicted—was that those instructions which he alleges the Commission to have violated were contained in the law. That is not a correct statement, as we have seen from the law itself. His next statement was that the Department of the Interior had prescribed certain regulations for the government of the Commission in its work, providing that those proceedings should be conducted in a certain way, and that those instructions were not followed. I know what the facts were, and that is why I call for this instruction. The instructions to which Mr. Ballinger has referred were issued on July 30, 1899, while these transactions occurred in the fall of 1898. That confirms what I stated this morning, that when the Commission proceeded in the fall of 1898 there were no departmental instructions; the Commission looked only to the language in the face of the law itself anda dopted that procedure and did those things which in its judgment ought to have been done.

Senator CLARK, of Wyoming. What is the date of those instructions?

Mr. CORNISH. July 25, 1899.

Senator CLARK, of Wyoming. Then those instructions were issued after the first tour of the Commission through the Chickasaw Nation?

Mr. CORNISH. Yes, sir.

Senator CLARK, of Wyoming. But before their second tour through the Choctaw Nation?

Mr Cornish I think it was while they were in the midst of their tour through the Choctaw Nation I remember all those circumstances very well, because I was with the Commission in 1899 as an attorney for the Chickasaws When the Commission proceeded in 1898, and when all of these transactions occurred, it was simply construing the law for itself, there were no instructions from the Department

Senator Clark, of Wyoming Let me ask you a question right there I want to get all these facts properly in my mind Are all these people who claim under Mr Ballinger all those who are confined to the Chickasaw people, or are they seeking to come in on the Choctaw rolls, which were not made until 1899?

Mr Cornish Some, I understand are claiming as Choctaws, but most of them as Chickasaws

Senator Clark of Wyoming When you say all were under the action of the committee in 1898, you do not mean to be understood as saying that he has none to come in under the Choctaws?

Mr Cornish No sir I am addressing myself to the incorrect statement that was made yesterday for the purpose of putting the Commission in a bad light I say that the Commission was proceeding upon its own construction of the law in its tour through the Choctaw Nation in 1898

Senator Clark, of Wyoming I did not understand Mr Ballinger to say anything about the tour through the Chickasaw Nation, or about its rolls, whether they were made in the Chickasaw or Choctaw Nation or wherever those people applied

Mr Cornish From the beginning of the Commissions tour through the Chickasaw Nation various people came in from other States and claimed that they had a right to apply as Indians, notwithstanding the fact that they had no tribal recognition, either by tribal enrollment or by being admitted by the Commission in 1896 But a controversy arose in the winter of 1898, and after they started out through the Choctaw Nation in 1899, then the question was submitted to the Department and these instructions, which I hold in my hand were given, and from that time the Commission followed those instructions and permitted everybody whether he be on a tribal roll or not to be heard They took down what he said, and submitted that case for the approval or disapproval of the Department as to whether they should or should not receive the application of the party

Senator Clark of Wyoming Let me interrupt you there—this matter covers so much ground, and I want to get distinctly in my mind the main points I understand you to assert now as a fact, that after these instructions were promulgated every person who applied to have his name entered on the rolls had his examination taken down in writing and preserved is that your recollection?

Mr Cornish That is my best information—not upon the merit of the claim but upon the proposition as to whether he was such a person as came within the jurisdiction of the Commission They heard him and took down his statement on the preliminary questions as to whether the Commission had or had not jurisdiction Then it was that Mr Van Devanter's opinion was rendered, which held that the Commission had no power to entertain an application on the merits The statement was taken down and reviewed by the Department on the preliminary question as to whether the Commission had jurisdiction. After hearing those facts, and it developed that he had not been on a tribal roll or had not been admitted under the law of 1896, the Commission held that it had no jurisdiction, and that construction of the law was held by Mr. Van Devanter.

Senator CLARK, of Wyoming. But in all the cases this preliminary examination was held as a permanent record?

Mr. CORNISH. Yes, sir.

Senator BRANDEGEE. But the examination did not go into the fact of whether he had any Indian blood in him or not?

Mr. CORNISH. Not upon the preliminary question, no; that was one of jurisdiction, as to whether he was such a person as came within the jurisdiction of the Commission, the requirement being that he must be in one of two classes—either upon a tribal roll or admitted by the Commission in pursuance of the jurisdiction of 1896. That meets the contention that the Commission was violating the law or ignoring its instructions in the fall of 1898.

Now, the way the Commission did proceed in 1898 was to receive the applications of persons who applied; if he came within the jurisdiction of the Commission, if he applied as an Indian, and a preliminary examination of the roll was made and it appeared that his name was on one of the tribal rolls, or that he had been admitted in 1896, the Commission had jurisdiction, and his application was placed on what was called a field or census card. Those cards are complete and thorough; they contain the name of the person, post-office address, age, name of father, name of mother, degree of blood, and the reference to the tribal roll upon which his name appears.

That is the record which the Commission did make in pursuance of that requirement of law, which says that the Commission shall make such rolls descriptive of the persons thereon. That is what it did under its construction of the law of 1898.

Now objection is made upon the ground (evidently for the purpose of putting the Commission in a bad light) that it did not take full and complete stenographic notes of the proceedings. The evidence of the applicants which was given to the Commission, or to the clerks of the Commission, which evidence or which testimony or which information went upon the face of these cards, was given under oath. Each applicant was put under oath, and the application of the applicant is not found in the brief stenographic notes to which reference has heretofore been made, but upon the field or census card which the Commission has made and kept, which was submitted to you yesterday. As I have said, it contained the name of the applicant, his age, post-office address, degree of Indian blood, if he be an Indian; and practically the same card was made use of in the enrollment of freedmen, except that that card contained the additional information as to the parents of the applicant and the particular Indian who was the owner of the ancestor through whom freedmen applicant claimed.

So much for that, as to the proceedings of the Commission under the law of 1898. I do not believe after an examination of these facts presented by the subcommittee in the Indian Territory, and here presented, that the conclusion can be fairly reached that the Commission did not exercise its very best judgment in an entirely proper way in the administration of the law of 1898 in the making up of those rolls The instructions which I have reference to were brought about by the insistent bombardment of the Commission by thousands—and since that time, scores of thousands—of persons who came in from the surrounding States Those instructions were brought about by those persons who came in from the surrounding States, who claimed to be Indians, but who did not come within the jurisdiction of the Commission, because they were not on the tribal rolls, and had not been admitted by the Commission in 1896

Now, the statement has been made that the law itself did not require the applicant to make an application that the duty rested upon the Commission to see to it that the application of every person who, upon any theory of the law had a right to apply should be brought in and the application made That view of the law can not be sustained The law of 1898 does not say in so many words that the applicant shall make a personal application The law of 1898 does not say that I have referred to that several times, and shall only do so now for the purpose of bringing out this particular point:

Said Commission shall make such rolls descriptive of the persons thereon so that they may be thereby identified and it is authorized to make a census of each of said tribes, etc

Under that they sent out notices to all who wished citizenship, and voluntary applications were made by every person claiming to be a citizen, and by everybody claiming to be a freedman, so there is no particular profit now in our showing what the duty of the Commission was The Commission construed that law and issued notices requiring persons to meet them at its apartments unless they were ill or infirm, and then some means were found by a member of the Commission going to the residence of any person who was physically disabled, and unable to come before the Commission But they construed that law to mean that those people should come before it and make application, and that was done, not only by the Indians but by all the parties represented by opposing counsel at the time

Senator BRANDEGEE If that is so, if a man appeared there, whether you call him an applicant or claimant, or a man who wanted to get enrolled and did not know which roll he ought to go on, but appeared there, is it not a fact that under these instructions contained in that act the Commission ought to have inquired about the amount of Indian blood he had in him for the purpose of determining which roll to put him on?

Mr CORNISH Perhaps we may at this time say that the Commission might have done something which they did not do If a man presented himself—if he was as black as the ace of spades, and said to the Commission "I am an Indian and have a right to be enrolled as an Indian," it was certainly the duty of the Commission to look into that matter to determine whether it had jurisdiction over him.

Senator BRANDEGEE I understood you to say as a matter of fact that the Commission did not make any inquiries as to the quantity of Indian blood in the applicant, and I understand that the testimony there is that in a great many cases represented by Mr Ballinger the quantum of Negro blood is much larger than the quantum of Indian blood, and in such cases if the applicant resembled an Indian more than a Negro, would they not ask him something about the amount of Negro blood instead of directing him to the freedmen tent?

Mr Cornish As I understand it, the first proper inquiry of the Commission would be to determine whether they had jurisdiction over that person The question of blood would not arise on the preliminary examination The first inquiry would be "Are you within our jurisdiction as an Indian? Are you in the tribal roll, or were you admitted by the Commission in 1896?" The rolls were before them, if a man said "I am an Indian," the first duty of the Commission would be to examine the roll to see if his name was on that roll, or to examine its records of 1896 to see if he had been admitted to those rolls in 1896 I am assuming now that he was not in either of those classes, then it developed that he was not within the jurisdiction of that Commission, and that would have ended the inquiry, upon the construction of the law placed upon it by Mr Van Devanter, and the law enacted the next year

Senator Clark, of Wyoming Now, as a matter of fact, the Indian rolls show a considerable number of people who had in their veins Indian blood

Mr Cornish Yes, sir, the statement has been made that there is a desire on the part of the Indians, and those representing the Indians, to discriminate against those Indians because of their Indian blood There could not be a more unfair statement than that There are many persons in the Choctaw and Chickasaw nations who are citizens and who are possessed of some negro blood That does not of itself bar them

Senator Long Under what circumstances are they put on there?

Mr Cornish They are put on by the Commission

Senator Long When are they put on and when rejected?

Mr Cornish The test is whether they are on the tribal roll, whether or not they have been recognized as Indians and their names appear on the tribal rolls Now, if a negro man is or should be married to an Indian woman, their children, notwithstanding the fact that they are children possessed of negro blood, would be entitled to enrollment as Indians if they had been placed on the rolls by the Indians

Senator Long And the tribes put such on the roll?

Mr Cornish Yes, sir, in many cases

Senator Long But suppose he had married a woman who had been a slave in the tribe contrary to the tribal law?

Mr Cornish The tribal custom, which is universal, and which has always been followed, would have intervened there and that child would have followed the status of the mother The mother is possessed and in the enjoyment of rights of Chickasaw citizenship in the tribe, that of freedmen, and the child would have undoubtedly been enrolled as a freedman

The statement that there is a desire on the part of the Choctaw and Chickasaws to discriminate against these persons because of their negro blood is absolutely untrue, because there are persons in the Choctaw and Chickasaw nations who are on the tribal roll and who are possessed of some negro blood I do not think that marriage and legitimacy of issue was presented when you were in the Indian Territory, but the Choctaw and Chickasaw nations have preserved their blood pure and uncontaminated, in so far as the colored race is concerned.

Their blood has been preserved with as much purity as in any other southern community. The negroes were their slaves, and they regarded them just as the slaves were in the South, except they have received vastly more benefits than in any other southern community, because of the property that was conferred on them. There has not only not been any discrimination so far as the Choctaws and the Chickasaws are concerned against their slaves, but they have done more for their slaves than is the case in any other southern community.

Senator McCumber. They did it more because of a pressure on the part of the Government as a punishment for taking sides with the Confederacy?

Mr. Cornish. Possibly; I do not know anything about the object of the treaty of 1866, but I say frankly if the Indians had been left to the entire control of the matter, I doubt very much if they would have given their slaves property valued at many millions of dollars. But the Government of the United States insisted that they do that. They agreed to it and have carried it out, and their freedmen, or their slaves, have been vastly more benefited under the peculiar conditions existing in that community than in any other southern community.

Senator La Follette. On the subject of that law of 1898, and I ask for information, was the Commission clothed with power to issue process to bring in those people?

Mr. Cornish. Yes, sir.

Senator La Follette. Could they summon them? I mean with reference to examination to ascertain their proper status, and whether they were entitled to enrollment?

Mr. Cornish. There was such a provision either under this law or a later law.

Senator La Follette. You do not think that was under the law of 1898?

Mr. Cornish. I do not think there was anything in the law of 1898 to that effect; possibly so.

Senator La Follette. If there was a provision there clothing them with that power, it would appear, would it not, as though it had been contemplated that they ought to search them out?

Mr. Cornish. Not when we consider the later law. I was coming to the law that was passed in the next year.

Senator Brandegee. They were directed to make a census of them.

Mr. Cornish. Yes, sir.

Senator La Follette. It was either in this hearing or some hearing that was held last session, in which I understood that they had the right to issue summons and subpoenas, and to attach their persons in order to bring them for such examination, and carry out the requirements of the law in completing the enrollment, whether they wanted to be enrolled or not.

Mr. Cornish. I am sure there was a provision in one of the later laws; when the whole work was about to be closed there was a provision requiring them to bring in such as had not presented themselves. If there was any doubt about the construction of the act of 1898, as to which of those persons were required to make applications, and that the Commission was not of its own motion required to beat the brush and figure out for them what their rights were—if there is any doubt on that proposition I think it is only necessary to refer to the law of 1900, which makes reference in terms to applications which shall be made by the applicants themselves. The act of May 31, 1900, says:

> The said Commission shall continue to exercise all the authority heretofore conferred upon it by law. But it shall not receive, consider, or make any record of the application of any person, etc.

That is the language used in the law of 1900 with regard to applications.

The law of 1902, section 27——

Senator WARNER. Is this the supplemental agreement?

Mr. CORNISH. This is section 27 of the act of 1902, known as the "Supplementary agreement:"

> The rolls of the Choctaw and the Chickasaw citizen and Choctaw and Chickasaw freedmen shall be made by the Commission to the Five Civilized Tribes in strict compliance with the act of Congress approved June 28, 1898 (30 Stat. L., 495), and the act of Congress approved May 31, 1900 (31 Stat. L., 221), except as herein otherwise provided.

Now, you will understand that up to the time the treaty of 1902 was adopted the Commission had not made the rolls. The Commission had only gone out into the field at various times and upon various occasions and in various ways, and gotten together these applications and the testimony, the crude material from which the rolls could be made. The roll was not made and completed under the law of 1898 or the law of 1900, but the provision for the completion of the rolls and the definition of the final authority of the Commission for the completion of that roll, and the prescribing of the manner in which it should be made, is contained in the treaty of 1902, under which the citizenship business was intended to be closed, and that said that the Commission should make the roll in accordance with the laws of 1898 and 1900. In section 34 of the same act, July 1, 1902, it is also provided:

> During the ninety days first following the date of the final ratification of this agreement the Commission to the Five Civilized Tribes may receive applications for enrollment only of persons whose names are on the tribal rolls, but who have not heretofore been enrolled by said Commission, commonly known as "delinquents," and such intermarried white persons as may have married recognized citizens of the Choctaw and Chickasaw nations in accordance with the tribal laws, customs, and usages on or before the date of the passage of this act by Congress, and such infant children as may have been born to recognized and enrolled citizens on or before the ratification of this agreement; but the application of no person whomsoever for enrollment shall be received after the expiration of said ninety days.

That is the provision of the law which fixes the 25th of December, 1902, as the final date on which applications may be received.

Senator LA FOLLETTE. If I may interrupt you, this memorandum has been handed to me and is marked as a part of the act of June 28, 1898. I will just read the paragraph to bring the matter to your attention in this connection:

> Said Commission shall make such rolls descriptive of the persons thereon so that they may be thereby identified, and it is authorized to make a census of each of such tribes, or to adopt any other means by them deemed necessary to enable them to make such rolls. They shall have access to all rolls and records of the several tribes, and the United States Court in the Indian Territory shall have jurisdiction to compel the officers of the tribal governments and the custodians of such rolls and records to deliver them to said Commission, and on their refusal or failure to do so to punish them as for

contempt, as also to require all citizens of said tribes, and persons who should be enrolled, to appear before said Commission for enrollment at such times and places as may be fixed by said Commission, and to enforce obedience of all others concerned, so far as the same may be necessary, to enable said Commission to make rolls as herein required and to punish anyone who may in any manner or by any means obstruct said work

This bears upon the question that I asked you before, as to whether there was not some obligation on the part of the Commission; that was not the question, the question was as to whether they did not have authority, and whether that did not imply an obligation that they should compel attendance and enforce obedience of all others concerned in the making of those rolls

Mr CORNISH Yes, sir, undoubtedly If any person had not made application the Commission would, under that provision of the law, have had power to enforce their attendance by process of the United States courts

Senator LA FOLLETTE Would it not appear to be the spirit if not the letter of that statute that they should exert themselves to make a complete roll of all persons concerned?

Mr CORNISH That they were undoubtedly required to do in the final completion of the work There were persons known as "delinquents," that is, after the Commission had operated in the country for five or six years there were Indians who did not look with favor upon the action of the Government of the United States, and there were many who even up to the time the work was closed refused to present themselves, and their attendance was compelled under either that provision or some later provision of law The Commission had undoubtedly the power to see to it that the persons who were entitled should be brought in

Now, these proceedings having been taken as stated and these particular applicants having voluntarily presented themselves a discussion of what the power of the Commission was with reference to any delinquents or persons who did not present themselves with an application would have very little application, or practically no application, so far as those persons are concerned, because they presented themselves every man, woman, and child presented himself voluntarily listed for enrollment as freedmen, and was subsequently enrolled by the Commission as freedmen, and for five long years—from 1898 until 1903—nothing was done, and nothing was said with reference to the existence in anybody's mind as to doubt of what their rights were During that time their enrollment was completed by the Commission to the Five Civilized Tribes and the Secretary of the Interior They were placed on a roll of freedmen and that was approved They presented themselves to the land office and voluntarily asked that the allotments to which they were entitled, to wit, 40 acres, be set apart for them. they were set apart for them, and after the work of the Government was practically completed under existing law then it was suggested by some one that those people had rights, and the case was referred to Mr Campbell, and the extraordinary decision, to which I have referred, was made After that decision was made these applications, aggregating some 1,500 persons, were filed with the Commission to the Five Civilized Tribes and are there now

This decision of Mr Campbell was in what is known as the Joe and Dillard Perry case In that case there was some contention that those children were legitimate children. That was the evidence on which Mr. Campbell passed. The alleged father of the children was a Chickasaw Indian and the woman was a negro woman and a freedman, with her status fixed as such and in the enjoyment of her status. She had applied for the enrollment of herself as a freedman and for the enrollment of those children as freedmen, and their rights had been fixed and had stood for more than five years before this idea was suggested. Then it was that upon those facts the decision of Mr. Campbell was rendered. There was some contention in this case that there had been a legal marriage between Perry and this woman. The children had been begotten, and this relation existed, and the authorities of the United States were to proceed against them. They were to be taken to Paris, Tex., for trial, and it was stated by the woman that about that time some sort of marriage ceremony had taken place. It was on that state of facts that the decision in the Joe and Dillard Perry case was rendered.

Senator McCumber. That decision which was rendered admitted them to citizenship?

Mr. Cornish. Yes, sir.

Senator McCumber. Although they were the children of a slave mother?

Mr. Cornish. Yes, sir.

Senator McCumber. That is contrary, of course, to your contention.

Mr. Cornish. It is contrary to the laws, customs, and usages of the tribes.

Senator McCumber. On what did he base that decision?

Mr. Cornish. It is just as broad as language can make it. He held in effect that the physical progeny—I use that because in this instance I think it is more descriptive than any term I can use—that the physical progeny of an Indian man, without reference to circumstances, and without reference to legitimacy or illegitimacy—if the physical fact be established that the child was begotten by the Indian man—that that entitled the child to enrollment as an Indian.

Senator Clark. of Wyoming. That would be a descendant?

Mr. Cornish. Yes, sir; according to Campbell.

Senator Long. Under the treaty of 1830?

Mr. Cornish. Yes, sir. Now, the committee will understand that our complete answer to this is that the word "descendants" or the construction given of the treaty of 1830, is entirely met and negatived by the use of the words "heirs and successors" in the treaty of 1855 and by the subsequent treaties of 1898 and 1902, which provide that the Commission to the Five Civilized Tribes and the Secretary of the Interior shall have no power to enroll any person unless that name appears on some one of the tribal rolls which were made in accordance with the laws, usages, and customs of the tribes.

Congress never intended to deprive the tribes in the making of rolls and of the protection of their own laws, customs, and usages.

Senator Warner. I understood you to say a few moments ago that Congress would have had the power to authorize a roll to be made up of that class of Choctaws and Chickasaws if they saw fit, whether full blood or half-breed.

Mr. Cornish. I stated my belief that the courts would sustain that power if Congress saw fit to exercise it. Congress has never exercised that power, and I do not believe it will do so.

Senator McCumber Was not that case which was before the Supreme Court a similar case to determine that same question?

Mr Cornish No, sir. This decision of Mr Campbell's is one of many decisions which have been rendered by Mr Campbell in recent years The select committee is of course in full possession of my views with reference to the weight that should be given to Mr Campbell's decision

Senator Brandegee That decision has been affirmed by the Attorney-General, has it not?

Mr Cornish No, sir

Senator Long Has it been submitted to the Attorney-General?

Mr Cornish No, sir, we have tried to have it submitted to the Attorney-General but that permission was specifically denied by the Secretary of the Interior

Senator Clark, of Wyoming Was that one of the cases that you asked to be submitted recently?

Mr Cornish No, sir

Senator Clark, of Wyoming You have never tested or sought to test this decision before the Attorney-General?

Mr Cornish No, sir, because if this committee and Congress should agree with us on this presentation of the matter that the law as it stands should not be changed, it is not a matter of any consequence because there is no power to pass on these applications

Senator Clark, of Wyoming And on your theory, if Congress admits these people to citizenship their influence would have no legal weight with the Attorney-General?

Mr Cornish No, if Congress should exercise the power to provide an enrollment of these people, of course none of the opinions of the executive officers would be of benefit to us

Senator McCumber I want to call your attention to a statement in a very late letter from the Commissioner in which he says

The Supreme Court of the United States in the case of the Chickasaw Freedmen v The Choctaw Nation and Chickasaw Nation (193 U S 115) held that the Chickasaw freedmen were not citizens of that nation and that whatever right they have to share in the distribution of the Choctaw and Chickasaw nations is by virtue of the operation of the act of July 1, 1902, and not independently thereof

Mr Cornish Yes, sir Are you familiar with that decision?

Senator McCumber I am not, I have not read it

Mr Cornish That is a case which was taken to the Supreme Court of the United States to determine the question as to whether or not the Chickasaw freedmen were entitled to the 40 acres of land under the treaty of 1866 You understand that in the treaty of 1898 it was agreed that Chickasaw freedmen should be enrolled, but the question of law as to whether they were entitled to that 40 acres of land should be determined later It was submitted to the Court of Claims under the treaty of 1902, and the decision to which you have reference is the affirmance by the Supreme Court of the United States of that decision

Senator McCumber But whether it is in direct issue or not, this case seems to have held that the Chickasaw freedmen were not citizens of that nation

Mr Cornish I do not see that that has any application because that decision bore entirely on the question of the rights of these people as freedmen The question was whether they had been adopted under the treaty of 1866 as freedmen. We contended that because of the fact that the freedmen had not been adopted the Chickasaws were entitled to pay for those lands.

Senator LONG. And the Supreme Court sustains that?

Mr. CORNISH. Yes, sir; and the Government of the United States will be called upon to pay——

Senator McCUMBER. Then I understand you to say that those words could not be held as res judicata of that subject?

Mr. CORNISH. No, sir; because the citizenship claim of these persons as Indians was not involved in that case. The word "citizenship," as used there and as has been used by the counsel for the Government, means that the right as freedmen was considered a limited citizenship. They made use of the term citizenship and that is the reason why the Supreme Court of the United States made use of that term. It had no reference to the claim of these people, now that they are citizen Indians.

Now, I shall further refer to this decision of Mr. Campbell. He has rendered many decisions in recent years, and if the committee were willing to listen to a long discussion of that matter I could convince you that this decision of Mr. Campbell is not entitled to that weight which would cause this committee or Congress to reverse the work of the Government in citizenship matters for the past ten years and to deprive the tribes of the protection of their own laws, customs, and usages which have grown up for their own protection and which the Government of the United States must follow in the making of these citizenship rolls.

I do not think Mr. Campbell's decisions are entitled to that weight which would have that effect on Congress. Mr. Campbell has rendered several decisions, which, if they stand, will deprive the tribes of many millions of dollars. He has held that certain decisions of the Choctaw and Chickasaw citizenship court, which Congress created, and which cost the Government more than $50,000 in salaries and expenses, are void. He has held that certain final decisions rendered by that tribunal should not be observed, and that the persons thus denied should be enrolled by the Secretary of the Interior. He has held many other things which are wrong and disastrous to the tribes. The statement was made yesterday with regard to the Mary and Elizabeth Martin case. That court held that the white child of an intermarried white person was not entitled to citizenship, and that the right of an intermarried white person was a personal right, a right personal to the individual, and that it could not be forfeited. Now, the Choctaw and Chickasaw citizenship court held that, and Mr. Campbell has overruled that decision, and has held that a white man who marries an Indian woman and dies, that that confers——

Senator McCUMBER. If he marries a white wife they are both white.

Mr. CORNISH. Both white; Mr. Campbell held that that child, the child of two white people, is entitled to citizenship. The law was declared by the Choctaw and Chickasaw citizenship court, which I have always maintained is the superior citizenship tribunal of the United States. In 1896 the Commission acted upon questions of law, the United States court acted upon questions of law, the Secretary of the Interior acted upon questions of law, and, finally, in 1902, after the citizenship matters had gone on for years and years, they were all at sea and Congress in its wisdom saw fit to create the Choctaw and

Chickasaw citizenship court   While its jurisdiction was limited to a trial and disposition of the cases arising under the act of June 10, 1896, yet we have always contended that the declarations of law by that court should be followed by the Commission of the Five Civilized Tribes and by the Secretary of the Interior   It was created for the purpose of summing up all these conflicting decisions, and we contend that its declarations of law should be followed in parallel cases

The departmental procedure is that when a decision is rendered by a subordinate officer of the Interior Department or any other Department, each Department having its Assistant Attorney-General, it is usual if it is felt that rights have been violated to ask the head of the Department to certify the question of law in that case to the Attorney-General of the United States

That was done in Indian citizenship up to a year ago, and we have had controversies with the Secretary of the Interior   We felt that the rights of the Choctaws and the Chickasaws were not only violated but outraged, and we filed a motion for a reconsideration of those decisions   They were thoroughly argued, but the decisions were adhered to   Then we addressed a letter to the Secretary of the Interior imploring him not on our own account, but on account of the vast interests that we represented, that he do the very reasonable and usual thing by referring these decisions to the Attorney-General for review by him of the decisions of the subordinate of the Attorney-General, and the Secretary of the Interior declined to do that

Senator McCumber   May I ask you one or two questions that follow on there?   Under the Indian law if a white man married an Indian woman, would that make him become a citizen of the tribe?

Mr Cornish   Yes, sir

Senator McCumber   If the woman died he still became a citizen of the tribe?

Mr Cornish   Yes, sir

Senator McCumber   If he remained single he continued to be a citizen?

Mr Cornish   Yes, sir

Senator McCumber   If he married in the tribe he was a citizen?

Mr Cornish   Yes, sir

Senator McCumber   If he married out of the tribe, does that forfeit his citizenship?

Mr Cornish   No, sir, under the laws of the tribe it did, but the Choctaw and Chickasaw citizenship court held against us to that extent

Senator McCumber   Did the laws of the tribe provide ----

Mr Cornish   That his citizenship should be forfeited?   Yes, sir; that his citizenship should be enjoyed only as long as he did certain things—lived with his Indian wife and Indian family   If he abandoned his Indian wife, or after her death remarried, he forfeited his citizenship

Senator McCumber   Then if he was a white man and married into the tribe, by virtue of that marriage and married out of the tribe, he forfeited his citizenship?

Mr Cornish   Yes, sir

Senator McCumber   But if another Indian, member of the tribe, should marry out of the tribe, he did not forfeit his citizenship?

Mr Cornish   No, sir, the white spouse would come into the tribe

Senator LONG. Has that decision ever been submitted to the Attorney-General?

Mr. CORNISH. The decision of the citizenship court?

Senator STONE. Suppose a white spouse should marry outside? In the case of her Indian husband, according to the tribal law, he would forfeit his citizenship?

Mr. CORNISH. Either spouse.

Senator BRANDEGEE. If Mr. Campbell's opinion—the Assistant Attorney-General of the Department of Interior—is erroneous in so many cases in your opinion, why did you not ask to have it—in this Joe and Dillard Perry case—sent over for a review of these other cases?

Mr. CORNISH. For this reason: If it is the view of this committee and of Congress that the citizenship law with reference to applications should stand as it is now, without amendment, that would not be of any use or benefit, because, as the law stands now—these people, not having on file applications as Indian citizens—there is no power to pass on their applications upon their merits at this time.

Senator BRANDEGEE. I understand; but when you know that this application for the repeal of that legislation which bars these people was pending I should suppose that you would have wanted to have that decision reversed, or, in other words, to have two strings to your bow.

Mr. CORNISH. That would be a matter that we would certainly insist upon if there should be a disposition on the part of Congress to reopen the question.

It was said that the decision in the Mary and Elizabeth Martin case was the law now. That statement is not true. We succeeded in calling that case to the attention of the President of the United States. The ordinary course is to send these cases over to the Attorney-General for review. In this case the Secretary of the Interior positively and flatly declined to do that and said, "I will not only not certify the case to the Attorney-General for review but I will see to it that you do not take it to the Attorney-General for review."

We succeeded in calling the Martin case to the attention of the President, and he made a peremptory order calling on the Commissioner of Indian Affairs for a report, and the Attorney-General sustained us and the citizenship court, and thus Mr. Campbell was reversed.

Senator LONG. That refers to white children with no Indian blood in their veins?

Mr. CORNISH. Yes, sir; that is the only way we succeeded in getting a reversal in that particular case. That left various other cases.

Senator McCUMBER. Was not that decision a clear recognition of the right of the tribes to govern their own citizenship?

Mr. CORNISH. I think so. We have taken some steps within the last two weeks to call these other cases to the attention of the President of the United States, and I think he will take the same action as to those cases that he did in the Mary and Elizabeth Martin case.

Senator LONG. What do those other cases cover?

Mr. CORNISH. The finality of the decrees of the Choctaw and Chickasaw court. In other words, there are certain persons in what is known as the West case who were denied by the citizenship court, and the decision became final under the law   Now Mr Campbell holds that such decision was without jurisdiction   We are asking that the question of law as to whether the decision of 1902 was final and should be observed be passed upon by the Attorney-General

Senator SUTHERLAND On what ground did Mr Campbell hold the decisions of the citizenship court invalid?

Mr CORNISH Upon the alleged ground that as to these persons who were passed on by the citizenship court, their names were included or appeared upon one of the tribal rolls, and under the law of 1896 the Commission to the Five Civilized Tribes acquired jurisdiction only of those persons who were not on the tribal rolls

Senator SUTHERLAND Then he held that the citizenship court had erred in that particular case, and not that the court was without power?

Mr CORNISH He held that in such a case the court was without jurisdiction

Senator SUTHERLAND Not without jurisdiction generally?

Mr CORNISH No, sir, that decision affected perhaps two or three hundred individual persons

Now, in order that you may understand the matter a little more fully, his decision was, in the West case, that since the names of these particular persons appeared on some one of the tribal rolls of the tribes, that none of the tribunals of the Government, the Commission in 1896, nor the United States courts that followed, nor the citizenship court ever acquired jurisdiction of them, for the reason that the tribal rolls as then existing "are hereby affirmed "

If the law of 1896 had stood, and there had been no amendment of that law by Congress, there certainly would be ground for contending that his decision was correct, but the law of 1897 defines the "rolls of citizenship " The rolls of citizenship were confirmed in the law of 1896, but the act of June 7, 1897, says

"That the words 'rolls of citizenship' as used in the act of June 10, 1896,   *   *   *   shall be construed to mean the last authenticated rolls of each tribe which have been approved by the council of the nation   *   *   * "

There are no rolls in the Choctaw and Chickasaw nations so approved, as required by these acts, and his conclusion is therefore necessarily erroneous

When those two laws are considered together and the light of the facts as to the tribal rolls the conclusion is reached that there are no rolls which were without inquiry by the Commission in 1896, and therefore no persons who were without its jurisdiction

Now, all this is in response to the suggestion that the Mary and Elizabeth Martin case was the law of the land, and had never been reversed The case was taken to the Attorney-General of the United States and was reversed, and the decision of the citizenship court was upheld and these persons denied

Now, when this Joe and Dillard Perry case was argued, we filed a motion to reopen the case and the original decision was adhered to Then it developed that these persons had not made the application which was required of all citizens of the Choctaw and Chickasaw nations under the provisions of the act of July 1, 1902 That is the law under which it was proposed to close citizenship matters, and provided that the application must be filed with the Commission by the 25th of December, 1902. Those persons were in the perfectly satisfactory enjoyment of their rights as freedmen at that time. They were in, as I say, the perfectly satisfactory enjoyment of their status as freedmen, and no applications were made, and as the law stands there is no power to pass on their applications as citizens.

Now, it was urged at the last session that you should give them some relief.

Senator Long. It later developed in that case that there was an application.

Mr. Cornish. In the Joe and Dillard Perry case in this way, and I beg the committee's pardon for taking up so much time, but if you wish me to make that point clear now I can. The individual persons in the Joe and Dillard Perry case have now been enrolled, because, as we show, under the law of 1902 there had been no applications for them under that law, and it is further shown that these particular persons had made application to the Commission under the law of 1896.

The jurisdiction of the Commission under the law of 1896 no more parallels the jurisdiction of the Secretary under the later laws than the jurisdiction of the mayor's court of the city of McAlester parallels the jurisdiction of this committee. The jurisdictions thus conferred are diametrically opposite, as opposite as jurisdictions could be. Under the law of 1896 the jurisdiction of the Commission was to admit to citizenship those persons who were not on tribal rolls, those persons who wished to be added to the tribal rolls from the outside and who wished to have conferred on them a tribal status and be placed on the rolls. Now that was the jurisdiction under the law of 1896.

The jurisdiction of the Commission and of the Secretary of the Interior under the later laws is just the opposite; it is to make up from the tribal rolls a correct roll. When it developed that the Joe and Dillard people had not made application in accordance with the law of 1902, then they began to cast around and see if there was not something in existence which could be construed into an application. So they found that application had been made by those persons in 1906 and Mr. Campbell held——

Senator Long. That is, they applied as Indians and citizens?

Mr. Cornish. Yes, sir. Now, Mr. Campbell held that that is such an application as may be considered an application within the meaning of the law of 1902, and the Joe and Dillard Perry people have been enrolled. I have not received a copy of the opinion, but I understand that the decision has lately been rendered.

But as to the great body of these people, there is no contention that they did make application within the time required by the law for their enrollment as Indians, and upon the suggestion of that of course they were out; and the contention was presented at the last session of Congress that steps should be taken to relieve them from that situation. Now, this committee did not feel and Congress did not feel that you could or would, or that it would be wise to reopen the matter as they wished it reopened. They contended, as they are contending now, that they had all along been asserting rights as citizens; that their enrollment had been over their protest, notwithstanding the fact that they applied voluntarily in 1898, and that continued until, perhaps, a year and a half ago. Notwithstanding all of that, they contended before you a year ago that they had been surging about the

Commission always, and that there was ample evidence of the fact that they had made some application under the law of 1902, and you very generously gave them that relief and provided if it could be shown by any scrap of paper, it might be considered an application And so it was provided in section 4 of the act of April 26, 1906 —

That no names shall be transferred from the approved freedmen or any other approved rolls of the Choctaw Chickasaw Cherokee Creek or Seminole tribes respectively to the roll of citizens by blood unless the records in charge of the Commission to the Five Civilized Tribes show that applications for enrollment as a citizen by blood was made within the time prescribed by law by or for the party seeking the transfer—

That time was the 25th of December, 1902—

and said records shall be conclusive evidence—

That means that unless the records showed that application was made that would be conclusive against the applicant that it was not made—

Unless—

Now, here is the very broad provision that was inserted—

Unless it be shown by documentary evidence that the Commission to the Five Civilized Tribes actually received such application within the time prescribed by law

Now, that has been held by the Commission to mean the development of anything in black and white, anything which is convincing of the fact, any scrap of paper of any character which can be developed to show that these people were from 1898 to the 25th of December, 1902, asserting rights as Choctaw and Chickasaw Indians Mr. Ballinger's statement yesterday was that notwithstanding the broad and comprehensive provision of that law (which we feel ought not to have been passed), yet notwithstanding the extent to which you went in that law, the statement of Mr Ballinger was that not a single individual had been able to comply with that provision of that law

If those people were Choctaw and Chickasaw Indians and felt themselves under the treaties and laws to be entitled to citizenship as Indians if they, as they now assert, had surged about the Commission from 1898, through the years of 1899 and 1900, 1901, and 1902, would it not be reasonable for us to assume, and would it not be easy for those people to show, that there was some scrap of paper on the part of some of them to show that there was some effort to assert those rights? Yet, according to the statement of Mr Ballinger, notwithstanding this positive provision of the law of 1902, and notwithstanding the very broad interpretation of that law which the Commission has given, they fail to come within that provision

Senator McCumber I understood Mr Ballinger to say that they did have that evidence, but that by some construction of the Department they were not allowed to use it I do not know that I remember what it was

Mr Cornish. No, sir, in the Joe and Dillard Perry case they found this paper, which had been made under the law of 1896

Mr. Ballinger Will the committee allow me to make a brief statement?

The Chairman Yes, sir

Mr Ballinger My statement was this That that documentary evidence was now obtainable, that the application was made, but the application having been removed from the Commission to a United

States court, and not being now in the possession of the Commission they held that under that section they could not consider it.

Mr. CORNISH. Who holds that?

Mr. BALLINGER. The Commission holds it.

Senator LONG. To what United States court do you refer?

Mr. BALLINGER. The court of the southern district of the Indian Territory. These applications were made under the act of 1896 and transferred to the court.

Senator McCUMBER. Do you mean to the Commission to the Five Civilized Tribes?

Mr. BALLINGER. Yes, sir; it was made to the Commission to the Five Civilized Tribes under the act of 1896. An appeal was taken from the decision in that case to the court sitting in the southern district of the Indian Territory. The record was transmitted to that court. The docket entry of the Commission shows the receipt of this application, and yet the Commission holds that as the application itself is not in the possession of the Commission that it can not consider it. Just one word further. The Commissioner himself stated in his answer to the proceedings before the select committee that he has never construed or defined what documentary evidence was.

Mr. CORNISH. All the records of the United States courts for the central and southern district of the Indian Territory are in his possession now; the records are available. Under a law which this Congress passed every person has free access to those papers.

Senator STONE. There seems to be a dispute of fact here.

Mr. BALLINGER. There is no dispute about it.

Senator McCUMBER. Do you know of any reason why the Commissioner should refuse to receive the documentary evidence simply because the document was not in his physical possession but in the possession of the court?

Mr. CORNISH. I do not think that is so; I know of no reason why that should be done. I hope you will understand this; I do not think as a matter of law that if it should develop that there were in those records made up under the law of 1906 papers which were filed for the establishment of that right under that jurisdiction, if there are papers in those batches of papers which refer to every one of those applicants, I do not believe that those are such papers as would be considered documentary evidence, giving force to those applications under the laws of 1898, 1900, and 1902.

Senator BRANDEGEE. What difference does the temporary jurisdiction of the Commission make under either of those acts as to the application of a party claiming to go under the roll of Indians by blood as to which time it was made. If it was made when the Commission had one jurisdiction, why is not an application for a determination of his rights as a claimant of Indian blood to go on that citizenship roll which the Commission, exercising a subsequent jurisdiction, hold to be a continuing application; why do you claim that they should not so hold?

Mr. CORNISH. I do not think there is anything in common between the papers accumulated under a former law for one purpose and a subsequent law for another purpose.

Senator McCUMBER. These papers do not state under what law they said they would receive it. If there was documentary evidence, it meant evidence in a document, or a written instrument.

Mr. CORNISH. This view expressed by me is very largely academic. The decision is against me by the Commission. The Commission has held that if any sort of a document is found in these papers it must be considered an application.

Senator McCUMBER. What I want to get at is whether or not the Commission has recognized that to be a correct proposition of law and refused those papers.

Senator BRANDEGEE. Those papers were not presented, as the Commission held, and, if so, I would like Mr. Ballinger to read it. Do they hold that all documentary evidence must be in the physical possession of the Commission itself, and that it is not sufficient if that documentary evidence exists in the files of the United States court in the Indian Territory although the record of the Commission itself shows that there had been such an application made?

Mr. CORNISH. I do not think that they have so held.

Senator BRANDEGEE. I would like to have Mr. Ballinger read that.

Mr. BALLINGER. I will read the copy of the letter inclosed to the attorney in this case, signed by C. F. Larrabee, Acting Commissioner of Indian Affairs, dated December 3, 1906, in which he sets out the decision in this case.

Senator BRANDEGEE. That is addressed to whom?

Mr. BALLINGER. It is addressed to the honorable Secretary of the Interior. It is the decision of the Commission, affirmed and transmitted. It is as follows:

The records of the Commission and of his office failing to show that any application had been made for the enrollment of the persons named by Mr. Lee in his petition of February 12, 1906, as citizens by blood of the Chickasaw Nation, prior to December 25, 1902, the Commissioner says that Mr. Lee now seeks to invoke the aid of the records of the United States court for the purpose of showing that such an application was made under the provisions of the act of June 10, 1896.

Senator CLARK, of Wyoming. Who are the persons named?

Mr. BALLINGER. Calvin Newberry and his children. The Commissioner refers to this as Mr. Lee's petition. He filed it as attorney.

Senator STONE. Who is Mr. Lee?

Mr. BALLINGER. This is Mr. Lee sitting here.

Senator McCUMBER. Please read that again.

Mr. BALLINGER (reads):

The records of the Commission and of his office failing to show that any application had been made for the enrollment of the persons named by Mr. Lee in his petition of February 12, 1906, as citizens by blood of the Chickasaw Nation, prior to December 25, 1902, the Commissioner says that Mr. Lee now seeks to invoke the aid of the records of the United States court for the purpose of showing that such an application was made under the provisions of the act of June 10, 1896.

What higher records could be envoked than the records of the United States?

Senator LONG. Read what was done on that.

Mr. BALLINGER. He cites the fact that the Department held on May 25, 1906, in the Cherokee enrollment case——

Senator CLARK, of Wyoming. What did he hold in that Newberry case?

Mr. BALLINGER. He holds here that as that application does not appear of record——

Senator LONG. Where is that—that is what I want to hear.

Mr. BALLINGER. The Commissioner quotes from section 4 of the act of Congress approved April 26, 1906, as follows:

That no name shall be transferred from the approved freedmen, or any other approved rolls of the Choctaw, Chickasaw, Cherokee, Creek, or Seminole tribes, respectively, to the roll of citizens by blood unless the records in charge of the Commissioner to the Five Civilized Tribes show that application for enrollment as a citizen by blood was made within the time prescribed by law, or by or for the party seeking the transfer, and said records shall be conclusive evidence as to the fact of said application, unless it be shown by documentary evidence that the Commission to the Five Civilized Tribes actually received such application within the time prescribed by law.

Senator McCUMBER. That is a different thing entirely.

Mr. BALLINGER. It is in here.

Senator LONG. Proceed, Mr. Cornish.

Mr. CORNISH. I had just quoted Mr. Ballinger as stating on yesterday that this provision of this law, however broad it is, is of no benefit to him. If the fact should be established as to the papers filed with the Commission in 1896, as suggested, that would not affect a half a dozen people. That is of no general application, and whatever benefits this law confers upon him, such as he reads in this case, he would have those benefits undoubtedly under the decision of the Secretary of the Interior and the Commission at this time, notwithstanding our view, as stated before, that such papers should not be considered an application within this law. The Commission and the Secretary hold otherwise, and if that paper exists in that way, and if other papers exist such as those, those papers will be considered documentary evidence within the meaning of this law, and these persons will be considered as having gotten their application within the time, and their case will be passed upon as in the light of the Joe and Dillard Perry case.

His general statement was (excluding the people who may have applied in 1896) that this was of no benefit to him.

Now, I suggest that it does seem that if these people were surging around the Commission and the Secretary, from 1898 down to recent years, confident of their own right as Indians, and had been certain of that through all those years, it does seem under the very broad provision of this law that there should have been some record of these insistent applications on their part, and some of them could have come within the purview of this law.

Now, just a word with reference to marriage and divorce in the Choctaw and Chickasaw nations.

Senator STONE. If this amendment proposed by Mr. Ballenger should be agreed to by the committee and Congress, what would it open up? What proof would be required to establish it?

Mr. CORNISH. Simply the oral evidence of blood on the part of every individual who could establish by oral evidence, or who could procure evidence orally in any way of his Indian blood. This would absolutely destroy every safeguard given us by the customs and usages of the tribe, and every safeguard given us by the laws of 1898, 1900, and 1902; it would repudiate the obligation of the Government to observe the tribal rolls and the laws, customs, and usages in making up the tribal rolls. The subject could not possibly be opened any broader than is proposed.

Just a word with regard to marriage and divorce in the Choctaw and Chickasaw nations. The marriage relation is observed as strictly as it is in any surrounding State. The earliest Choctaw marriage law was in 1835, and their provision of laws has been continued from that time down to the present time. These laws, covering the whole subject of marriage, divorce, alimony, polygamy, adultery, legitimacy, and legitimacy of issue appear in certain printed volumes as follows: "Laws of the Choctaw Nation, 1869," "Laws of the Choctaw Nation, 1894," and "Constitution, Treaties, and Laws of the Chickasaw Nation, 1898," and are as follows:

LAWS OF THE CHOCTAW NATION, 1869

(Page 70.)

AN ACT Defining what constitutes lawful matrimony.

SEC. 1. *Be it enacted by the general council of the Choctaw Nation assembled,* That the following mode of matrimony shall be lawful in this nation, viz: the parties shall go before any captain or preacher of the gospel in the nation who shall ask the groom "Are you willing to marry this woman whom you hold by the hand as your lawful wife?" If he says yes, then the captain or the preacher of the gospel shall then ask the woman "Are you willing to become the wife of this man who holds you by the hand?" If she says yes, or be silent, he shall say "I pronounce you man and wife." *Provided,* All marriages previous to this act shall be valid and lawful, and all property shall upon the death of the husband descend to the wife and children of the deceased husband, and in case of the death of the wife the husband shall inherit the estate.

Approved October 8, 1835.

(Page 71.)

AN ACT Allowing the Choctaws to intermarry without any regard to distinction as to Iksa.

SEC. 5. *Be it enacted by the general council of the Choctaw Nation assembled,* That the custom of not intermarrying with their own Iksa among the Choctaw people shall forever be abolished, and all persons without any distinction of Iksa are left to make their own choice as to whom they shall marry.

Approved October 6, 1836.

(Page 93.)

AN ACT Declaring the punishment for separating man and wife.

SEC. 2. *Be it enacted by the general council of the Choctaw Nation assembled,* That from and after the passage of this act, any person who shall be found guilty of taking or separating a woman from her husband who was lawfully married, he or they so offending shall pay a fine of ten dollars which shall go to the district treasury, and the parties restored to each other if they wish it.

Approved October 12, 1847.

(Page 105.)

AN ACT Directing any person marrying runaway matches to be fined.

SEC. 13. *Be it enacted by the general council of the Choctaw Nation assembled,* That from and after the passage of this act that any captain or minister of the gospel, or any other person, who shall marry or join together in wedlock any runaway matches, shall be fined twenty-five dollars for every act they violate of the above law, and all such marriages shall not be considered lawful, and all fines imposed under this law shall go to the district in which such fine may be imposed.

Approved October 11, 1849.

S. Doc. 257, 59-2——5

(Page 105.)

AN ACT Declaring punishment for polygamy.

SEC. 14. *Be it enacted by the general council of the Choctaw Nation assembled,* That from and after the passage of this act that any person or persons who shall be convicted of the crime of polygamy, or of living with each other in adultery, shall be liable to indictment before any court in this nation, and fined not exceeding twenty-five dollars, nor less than ten dollars for each of such offences.

And be it further enacted, That after the passage of this act all person or persons who may be living together out of wedlock shall be compelled to be lawfully joined together, or the party refusing so to do, shall be indicted and fined not less than ten dollars, nor exceeding twenty-five dollars for every such offence.

And be it further enacted, That the informant in all such offences as above specified shall be entitled to and receive one-third of the fines that may be so collected, and, after deducting the fees of the district attorney, the remainder shall become district funds.

October 11, 1849.

(Page 106.)

AN ACT Compelling white man living with an Indian woman to marry her lawfully.

SEC. 15. *Be it enacted by the general council of the Choctaw Nation assembled,* That every white man who is living with Indian woman in this nation without being lawfully married to her shall be required to marry her lawfully or be compelled to leave the nation, and forever stay out of it.

Be it further enacted, That no white man who is under a bad character will be allowed to be united an Indian woman in marriage in this nation under any circumstances whatever.

Approved, October, 1849.

(Page 115.)

AN ACT Authorizing the judges and preachers of the Gospel to solemnize the rites of matrimony.

SEC. 28. *Be it enacted by the general council of the Choctaw Nation assembled,* That from and after the passage of this act it shall be lawful for all the judges of this nation and preachers of the Gospel to solemnize the rites of matrimony and issue certificates thereof, if required, and be allowed and receive for every such service two dollars, to be paid by the parties so joined together.

And be it further enacted, That the law passed in session 5th, section 3rd, so far as relates to the fees, be and is hereby repealed.

Approved Oct. 17, 1850.

(Page 116.)

AN ACT Providing at what age marriage may be contracted.

SEC. 29. *Be it enacted by the general council of the Choctaw Nation assembled,* That from and after the passage of this act that every male who shall have arrived at the full age of eighteen years, and every female who shall have arrived at the full age of sixteen years, shall be capable in law of contracting marriage. But if under these ages their marriage shall be void, unless free consent by the parents and relations or guardian have been first obtained.

Be it further enacted, That whoever shall contract marriage in fact contrary to the prohibition of the preceding section of this act, and whoever shall knowingly solemnize the same, shall be deemed guilty of high misdemeanor, and shall, upon conviction thereof, be fined or imprisoned at the discretion of the court.

Approved, October, 1850.

(Page 153)

AN ACT legitimatizing the children of William and Jane Guy

SEC. 21. Be it enacted by the General Council of the Choctaw Nation assembled, That from and after the passage of this act, Eliza Jane, Serena Josephine, William Malcom, Mary Angeline, James Henry Harris, Lucinda, and Douglas Jackson Guy, children of William Guy, are, and they are hereby declared to be the lawful heirs of Jane Guy, deceased, and William Guy, of Blue County, Pushamataha district of the Choctaw Nation.

Approved November 12, 1856.

— —

Page 204

AN ACT Introduced to enforce and declare what shall constitute an unlawful marriage, the crime of incest, etc.

SEC. 1. Be it enacted by the General Council of the Choctaw Nation, That the son shall not marry his mother.

The son shall not marry his stepmother.

The brother shall not marry his sister nor his sister's daughter.

The father shall not marry his daughter.

The father shall not marry his daughter's daughter.

The son shall not marry his father's daughter, begotten of his stepmother, nor his aunt, being his father's or mother's sister.

The father shall not marry his son's widow.

A man shall not marry his wife's daughter, or his wife's son's daughter's daughter, or his wife's son's daughter, and the like prohibition shall extend to females within the same degrees, and all marriages of the nature are hereby declared incestuous and void.

Approved 26th October, 1858.

— —

Page 343

AN ACT concerning divorce in general

SEC. 1. Be it enacted by the General Council of the Choctaw Nation assembled, That all marriages which are prohibited by law, on account of the consanguinity between the parties, or on account of either party having a former husband or wife then living, shall not be solemnized within this nation, and shall be void without any decree of divorce or other legal proceedings.

SEC. 2. Be it further enacted, That the circuit court in the county in which the plaintiff resides has jurisdiction of all cases of divorce, and of alimony and other matters connected therewith.

SEC. 3. Be it further enacted, That the petition for divorce must state the facts on account of which the plaintiff claims the relief sought, must state that he or she has been for the last six months a resident of the county, and that the application is not made through collusion or restraint, or any cause knowingly existing with the defendant, but in sincerity and truth for the purpose set forth in the petition; it must also be sworn to by the plaintiff.

SEC. 4. Be it further enacted, That divorces from the bonds of matrimony may be decreed against the husband in the following cases: First, when the defendant at the time of his marriage was impotent; second, when he had a lawful wife then living; third, when he has committed adultery subsequent to the marriage; fourth, when he willfully deserts his wife and absents himself without a reasonable cause for the space of one year; sixth, when after marriage he becomes addicted to habitual drunkenness; seventh, when he is guilty of such inhuman treatment as to endanger the life of his wife.

SEC. 5. Be it further enacted, That the husband may in all cases obtain a divorce from the wife for like causes.

SEC. 6. Be it further enacted, That if the defendant does not appear and answer the petition at the proper time, the court, if satisfied that the complainant is the injured party, may decree a dissolution of the marriage contract; or when the defendant can be found, it may, in its discretion, bring him or her in by attachment and compel him or her to answer.

SEC. 7. Be it further enacted, That when a divorce is decreed, the court may make such order, in relation to the children and property of the parties and the maintenance of the wife, as shall be right and proper: subsequent changes may be made by the court in these respects where circumstances render them expedient.

SEC. 8. *Be it further enacted*, That when a divorce is decreed, the parties shall have the right to divide such property equally that may have been jointly accumulated while living together.

SEC. 9. *Be it further enacted*, That no decree of divorce shall affect the legitimacy of any child begotten within the bonds of lawful wedlock.

SEC. 10. *Be it further enacted*, That all acts or parts of acts heretofore passed coming in any wise in conflict with the provisions of this act be, and the same are hereby repealed, and that this act take effect and be in force from and after its passage.

Approved, October 30th, 1860.

(Page 385.)

AN ACT Entitled An Act legalizing the heirs of Curtis Grubbs and Elizabeth McLaughlin.

SEC. 1. *Be it enacted by the General Council of the Choctaw Nation assembled*, That the children of Curtis Grubbs and Elizabeth McLaughlin are hereby rendered and made legal and legitimate children of the said parties in as full and efficient manner as if the same had been in legal wedlock.

SEC. 2. *Be it further enacted*, That said children—Mary Jane, Benjamin Forbis and Robert Grubbs, the issue of Curtis Grubbs and Elizabeth McLaughlin—are hereby rendered capable in law to inherit, take and receive any property or profit that they might or could have done were they born in legal wedlock.

SEC. 3. *Be it further enacted*, That this act take effect and be in force from and after its passage.

Approved, October 8, 1863.

LAWS OF THE CHOCTAW NATION, 1894.

(Page 24.)

Sec. 24, Article 7, Constitution of 1859.

Divorces from the bond of matrimony shall not be granted but in cases provided for by law.

(Durant—Page 205.)

SECTION VI.—*Polygamy and adultery.*

1. *Be it enacted by the general council of the Choctaw Nation assembled:* Any person or persons who shall be convicted of polygamy or living with each other in adultery, shall be liable to indictment before any court in this nation and fined not exceeding twenty-five dollars nor less than ten dollars for each of such offences. Any person or persons who may be living together out of wedlock shall be compelled to be lawfully joined together, or the party refusing so to do shall be indicted and fined not less than ten dollars nor exceeding twenty-five dollars for every such offence; and the informant in all such offences as above specified shall be entitled to and receive one-third of the fines that may be so collected, and after deducting the fees of the district attorney the remainder shall become county funds.

(Durant—Page 205.)

SECTION VII.—*Incest.*

1. *Be it enacted by the general council of the Choctaw Nation assembled:* The son shall not marry his mother; the son shall not marry his stepmother; the brother shall not marry his sister nor his sister's daughter; the father shall not marry his daughter; the father shall not marry his daughter's daughter begotten of his stepmother, nor his

aunt, being his father's or mother's sister; the father shall not marry his son's widow; a man shall not marry his wife's daughter, or his wife's daughter's daughter, or his wife's son's daughter, and the like prohibition shall extend to females within the same degrees, and all marriages of this nature are hereby declared incestuous. If any person shall marry within the degrees prohibited by law, on conviction thereof they shall be fined two hundred dollars, or each receive one hundred lashes well laid on their bare backs, and such marriage is declared incestuous and void. If any persons who have been divorced for incest shall, after such divorce, cohabit or live together as man and wife, such persons so offending shall be deemed guilty of incest and fined, on conviction, two hundred dollars, or receive two hundred lashes, during two days, well laid on the bare back, or both, at the discretion of the court.

(Durant—Page 206.)

SECTION VIII.—*Intermarriage between Choctaws and negroes.*

1. *Be it enacted by the general council of the Choctaw Nation assembled:* It shall not be lawful for a Choctaw and a negro to marry; and if a Choctaw man or Choctaw woman should marry a negro man or negro woman he or she shall be deemed guilty of a felony, and shall be proceeded against in the circuit court of the Choctaw Nation having jurisdiction the same as all other felonies are proceeded against, and if proven guilty shall receive fifty lashes on the bare back.

(Page 233.)

SECTION 1.—*Marriage.*

Be it enacted by the general council of the Choctaw Nation assembled, Every male who shall have arrived at the full age of eighteen years and every female who shall have arrived at the full age of sixteen years shall be capable in law of contracting marriage, provided no other legal prohibition exists. But if under these ages, their marriage shall be void, unless free consent by the parents and relations or guardian has been first obtained. Whoever shall contract marriage in fact contrary to the prohibition of this section, and whoever shall knowingly solemnize the same shall be both be deemed guilty, one or both, of high misdemeanor, and shall upon conviction thereof be fined or imprisoned, at the discretion of the court. It shall be lawful for all the judges of this nation and preachers of the gospel to solemnize the rites of matrimony and issue certificates thereof, if requested, and be allowed and receive for every such service two dollars, to be paid by the parties so joined together. All marriages which are prohibited by law on account of consanguinity between the parties or on account of either of them having a former husband or wife then living shall, if solemnized within this nation, be absolutely void, without any decree of divorce or other legal proceedings.

CONSTITUTION, TREATIES, AND LAWS OF THE CHICKASAW NATION
1899.

(Page 6.)

Section 15, article 1, constitution of 1867.

Neither polygamy nor concubinage shall be tolerated in this nation from and after the adoption of this constitution.

(Page 18.)

Section 4, general provisions of the constitution of 1867.

Divorces from the bonds of matrimony shall not be granted but in cases provided for by law by suit in the district court of this nation.

(Page 76)

AN ACT To record marriages, etc

SECTION 1 *Be it enacted by the legislature of the Chickasaw Nation,* That from and after the passage of this act all persons marrying in this nation shall have the same reported in the clerk's office of the county court in the county in which they may reside

SEC 2 *Be it further enacted* That all persons neglecting to record their marriages within one month from the time they are married shall be fined in a sum not less than five nor exceeding ten dollars at the discretion of the court having jurisdiction of the same

SEC 3 *Be it further enacted* That all fines imposed under this act shall be collected by the sheriff or constable by order of the county court in the county in which such violation may have occurred

SEC 4 *Be it further enacted* That all marriages in this nation shall be solemnized by any judge or ordained preacher of the gospel For every couple joined together in the bonds of matrimony the person pronouncing the ceremony shall for every such service receive the sum of one dollar from the persons joined together

SEC 5 *Be it further enacted,* That all persons who are living together out of wedlock shall be compelled by the county judge to be lawfully joined together in the bonds of matrimony and any person refusing to be lawfully joined together shall be compelled to pay a fine of not less than twenty-five nor exceeding fifty dollars

SEC 6 *Be it further enacted,* That the county judge shall cause all fines imposed under the above act to be collected by the sheriff or constable and when collected to be placed in the county treasury for county purposes

Approved October 12, 1876

    B F OVERTON, *Governor*

———————

(Page 78)

AN ACT To legalize marriages solemnized by licensed preachers

PREAMBLE

Whereas it is enacted in section 4 of the "Act to record marriages" that any judge of the Chickasaw Nation, or any ordained preacher of the gospel, shall have the power to perform the marriage ceremony,

And whereas many of our citizens have been united in the bonds of matrimony by preachers not ordained nor authorized to marry individuals by the regulations of the church to which such preachers belong,

And whereas the district court of the Chickasaw Nation in the county of Pontotoc, at the January term, did decide that all such marriages were authorized by the church to which such preachers belong and consequently both canonically and legally void,

And whereas the person so marrying, as well as the licensed preacher performing the ceremony, did the same in good faith and without any doubt whatever of the lawfulness of it

And whereas by the decision in question the parties living together are not husband and wife nor the children of such marriage legitimate Therefore

SEC 1 *Be it enacted by the legislature of the Chickasaw Nation,* That every marriage which has been solemnized by any U N ordained licensed preacher within the limits of the Chickasaw Nation before the passage of this act is hereby legalized and every child born in marriage the offspring of it is hereby declared to be legitimate and shall be entitled to all the rights privileges and immunities thereof, just the same as if the marriage ceremony had been performed by any lawful judge of this nation or any ordained preacher of the gospel, as contemplated in the 4th section specified in the preamble of this act

SEC 2 *Be it further enacted* That all marriages which may hereafter be solemnized by licensed preachers shall be lawful just the same as if the ceremony was performed by any ordained minister of the gospel or judge of this nation and this act shall be enforced from and after its passage

Approved, October 12, 1876

    B F OVERTON. *Governor.*

(Page 104)

AN ACT To prohibit polygamy

SEC 1 *Be it enacted by the legislature of the Chickasaw Nation.* That from and after the passage of this act no citizen of this nation shall be allowed more than one lawful, living wife or husband, and every person violating this act shall be deemed guilty of polygamy and shall be subject to indictment, trial, and punishment by the district court of the county where the offense may have been committed

SEC 2 *Be it further enacted,* That polygamy shall consist in being married by any judge of this nation or other person lawfully authorized to perform the marriage ceremony, to two or more men or women, as the case may be, the first husband or wife being still alive, and undivorced by the district court of this nation, and all such marriages shall be void from the beginning just the same as if they had not been solemnized, and no rights of citizenship whatever shall be acquired by such unlawful marriages

SEC 3 *Be it further enacted* That every person found guilty of polygamy shall be compelled to separate and remain apart until the disability is removed and shall pay the cost of the suit and be fined fifty dollars, one half of the fine when collected, shall go to the attorney prosecuting the suit, and the other half with the cost of the suit shall be paid into the national treasury by the collecting officer at the end of every fiscal quarter to be used for public purposes

SEC 4 *Be it further enacted* That should the party convicted of polygamy not be able to pay the fine and cost of suit then and in that case the party shall be committed to jail with hard labor for not less than one nor more than six months at the discretion of the court for the first offense, and for every succeeding offense the last-mentioned time of imprisonment and hard labor together with the aforementioned fine and costs shall be the punishment and they shall be collected by the provisions of the Act in relation to collection of bonds and fines "

Approved October 10, 1876

B F OVERTON *Governor*

(Page 112)

AN ACT In relation to marriages under Choctaw law

SEC 1 *Be it enacted by the legislature of the Chickasaw Nation* That from and after the passage of this act all persons that were married under the Choctaw law, or by mutual consent of parties who lived together as man and wife six months previous to the adoption of the constitution of the Chickasaw Nation dated August 30 1856 shall be compelled by the county judge to have the same established upon oath and recorded in the office of the county clerk

SEC 2 *Be it further enacted* That it shall be the duty of the county judges to notify the people of their respective counties of the passage of this act and any person or persons who refuse or neglect to have their marriage reported within three months after the passage of this act shall be compelled to pay a fine not less than five nor exceeding fifteen dollars at the discretion of the court

SEC 3 *Be it further enacted* That all fines imposed under this act shall be collected by the sheriff or constable, and be placed in the county treasury

Approved, October 17, 1876

B F OVERTON *Governor*

(Page 122)

AN ACT Concerning concubinage and adultery

SEC 1 *Be it enacted by the legislature of the Chickasaw Nation* That when any person having a wife or husband and shall be found living with or keeping another woman or man shall be deemed guilty of concubinage or adultery and shall be subject to indictment, trial and punishment in the district court of the county where the offense may have been committed

SEC 2 *Be it further enacted* That every person found guilty of concubinage or adultery shall be compelled to separate forever and remain apart and fined in the sum of fifty dollars and cost of suit, one-half of the said fine shall when collected go to the attorney prosecuting the suit and the other half to the national treasury for national purposes said costs and fine shall be collected as other fines and costs are

Approved October 17, 1876

B F OVERTON, *Governor*

(Page 224)

AN ACT In relation to divorce

SEC 1 *Be it enacted by the legislature of the Chickasaw Nation,* That the district court of the Chickasaw Nation shall hear and determine all suits for the dissolution of marriages. The courts aforesaid are hereby invested with full power and authority to decree divorces from the bonds of matrimony in the following cases that is to say In favor of the husband where the wife shall have been taken in adultery, or where she shall have voluntarily left his bed and board for the space of six months with the intention of abandonment, also in favor of the wife for the same offense

SEC 2 *Be it further enacted.* That a divorce from the bonds of matrimony may be decreed in the following cases Where either the husband or wife is guilty of excesses cruel treatment or outrages toward the other, if such ill treatment is of such a nature as to render their living together insupportable

SEC 3 (Provides for procedure and for rights of children and of each party)

SEC 4 *Be it further enacted,* That a divorce from the bonds of matrimony shall not in any wise affect the legitimacy of the children thereof and it shall be lawful for either party after dissolution of marriage to marry again

SEC 5 (Provides for taking of testimony and for appeals to supreme court)

SEC 6 (Refers to debts and community property of parties)

SEC 7 (Also refers to debts)

SEC 8 (Refers to costs of suit)

SEC 9 (Refers to collection of costs)

Approved October 12 1876

B F OVERTON *Governor*

Marriage licenses were issued, they are observed. Their requirements as to marriage and divorce are just as strong and as strictly observed, and as generally observed, as they are in connection with a like number of people in any surrounding State

Those people have lived there with their slaves always, and they have regarded their slaves just as the people of Arkansas Alabama, and the other Southern States. There have been no marriages between them and their slaves— I do not mean that there has not been a single instance—but I mean to say that it is against their laws, the laws have prohibited such marriages

Senator LONG Since when?

Mr CORNISH There has been considerable discussion as to when the first law in the Chickasaw Nation was passed. There is a law in the Choctaw Nation, the date of the passage of which does not appear, and it has been contended by many that there was a law passed in the Chickasaw Nation in the early seventies. But, be that as it may, a sentiment has existed, and that sentiment has been observed with practical unanimity by the Choctaws and Chickasaws, just as it has been observed by the other southern people in the surrounding States. So there has not been such a thing as marriage between Indians and freedmen women

Senator McCUMBER There is one law of this character, of October 30, 1888?

Mr CORNISH Yes, sir, that was the law to which you had reference yesterday

Senator McCUMBER No, that is not the one

Mr CORNISH There has been some discussion about marrying with persons of color, but the custom has existed, and it has been observed with almost universal unanimity. I do not mean to say that no one instance has occurred where a marriage ceremony has been performed between an Indian man and a negro woman, but I do say that the relations existing between the Choctaws and Chickasaws and their slaves, their freedmen, has been the same relation that has existed in other southern communities between the white people and the negroes, and to say that the marriage relation has been established in a general way between those Choctaw and Chickasaw women is not true and is not established by any evidence produced before this committee

Senator SUTHERLAND I thought some decision was referred to here from the supreme court of Alabama, which held that marriage was recognized where men and women simply lived together

Mr CORNISH That discusses the doctrine of common-law marriage

Senator SUTHERLAND I understand that they held in that decision that that form of marriage and form of divorce was recognized by the tribes

Mr CORNISH I am not familiar with that decision The Choctaws and Chickasaws left the State of Alabama in 1830, and any declaration which an Alabama court may have made with regard to an Indian who resided in the State of Alabama would not have any reference to the laws, customs, and usages of tribes in Indian Territory, where they have a written constitution and laws I do say that the relations existing between the Choctaws and Chickasaws have been exactly the same as the relation existing, and which is universal, between the southern people and the negroes in any other southern community, and any mixture of the races resulting in social ostracism has resulted just as completely and just as rapidly as in any other southern community in the United States

Senator BRANDEGEE There was no penalty, was there attached to that prohibiting intermarriage?

Mr CORNISH Yes, sir

Senator McCUMBER Yes it was made a felony

Senator BRANDEGEE I mean the statute of 1888

Senator LONG What does the statute say with reference to that?

Mr CORNISH I am not able to give a reference to the particular statute in the Chickasaw Nation

Senator CLARK, of Wyoming Is there anything in this law of 1888 which makes it a felony an intermarriage of this sort? Is there anything in the law as to the property rights of the children of such a marriage?

Mr CORNISH I have not the law before me

Senator LONG It is in the law of 1888, I think

Mr CORNISH Therefore, gentlemen, it comes down to this proposition I do not mean to say that there has not been a marriage ceremony performed at some time in an isolated case between an Indian man and a colored woman, but such a condition is as rare as it is in any other southern State

Senator LONG If there was such a marriage, how would the issue of such a marriage be treated by the court?

Mr CORNISH If the woman was a freedman, the issue would follow the status of the mother in pursuance of the customs and usages of the tribe, and become freemen and enjoy the rights of the mother

Senator LONG Has there been any departure from that rule?

Mr CORNISH Not so far as I know I know that has been the custom and usage

Senator STONE Suppose the mother was an Indian woman?

Mr CORNISH Then the progeny would be Indian, and would follow the status of the mother

Senator SUTHERLAND. Is that the rule in the Choctaw tribe, that the child follows the status of the mother and not the father?

Mr. CORNISH. If the mother is not in the enjoyment of citizenship rights, then the child would follow the status of the father, the test of all that being the existence of the tribal rolls themselves; the test of whether or not the child is legitimate, which the tribunals that Congress created are bound to follow, is an examination of the tribal rolls themselves.

Senator CLARK, of Wyoming. Suppose the father was an Indian and married a white woman, or had children by a white woman, the child would follow the status of the father?

Mr. CORNISH. Yes, sir; if it is a legitimate issue.

Senator CLARK, of Wyoming. Suppose the father was an Indian and married a free negro woman from Arkansas, or anywhere else, then what would be the status of the child; would it follow the status of the father?

Mr. CORNISH. I shall come directly to your question. I do not know of any instance of that kind, and I will say that if there are any such instances they are very isolated, very rare indeed; but in cases like that I would say, if that existed, it would result perhaps in social ostracism to the Indian man if the marriage was a marriage in good faith and the man lived, and they were in fact a family, and recognized by the father, then I would say he would have brought about their enrollment.

Senator CLARK, of Wyoming. Suppose the father was an Indian and the mother an Indian woman, and there had been no marriage, what would be the status of the children?

Mr. CORNISH. You have reference to a common-law marriage. If it was merely intercourse and the children were not recognized by the father——

Senator CLARK, of Wyoming. Suppose they were recognized by the father?

Mr. CORNISH. I would say he would have brought about their enrollment—found a way to bring their names on the tribal rolls.

Senator CLARK, of Wyoming. What would be their legal status?

Mr. CORNISH. If it is a common-law marriage within the requirements of the law as to marriages, they would be legitimate children.

Senator CLARK, of Wyoming. Suppose it was a common-law marriage between the Indian and a negro woman?

Mr. CORNISH. I do not know of any cases of that kind. I do not know that there any such instances, but I would say if it was in good faith a marriage, the children were legitimate, even in the absence of a marriage ceremony.

Senator STONE. Do you mean in the absence of a law?

Mr. CORNISH. The test of the whole matter would be the tribal rolls.

Senator CLARK, of Wyoming. No; that is not the test at all. The test is the customs of the tribe. That fixes the roll; the roll does not fix the custom of the tribe. Now, my question is—the meat of my question is—whether or not there is any difference in the status of the child when the father is an Indian, as to whether the mother of the child is a white woman or a negro woman; if it makes any difference with the status of the child.

Mr. CORNISH. I am not able to say, because the facts do not exist which you suppose; therefore, I have not had an opportunity to make inquiry into it. Those facts do not exist. I do not mean to say there is no such case in the many thousand people.

Senator CLARK, of Wyoming. These are all those cases of mixed Indian blood, where the mother is an Indian and the father is a black man. I supposed it was just the other way. I had supposed that in nearly all those cases the father was an Indian and the mother was a negro.

Mr CORNISH. Yes, sir, and the intercourse was wholly illegitimate, if there was the fact of the intercourse. Conceding the fact that those persons were begotten by Indian men in an intercourse which had no relation to a marriage, or any relations of husband and wife, they are illegitimate just the same as the mulattoes who have grown up in the South, that is all. The most that can be said is that it can not be contended that those children are the result of marriages in any sense of the word.

Senator CLARK, of Wyoming. I am afraid I have been groping in the dark. I had supposed that on those rolls there was some people with negro blood in them.

Senator LONG. On the Indian roll?

Senator CLARK, of Wyoming. On the Indian roll.

Mr CORNISH. That is true, it would not be impossible. I stated it, but it did not arise in the case you stated. If there be an Indian woman, she is in the enjoyment of her status, and if she had intercourse with a negro man the child would follow the status of the mother and be enrolled as an Indian.

Senator WARNER. Have you not stated that there are some cases where a full-fledged Indian married a negro woman?

Mr CORNISH. No, I stated as a general proposition that there was a considerable number of persons enjoying citizenship who were possessed of negro blood, but I did not state how that condition arose. It did not and could not have arisen under the laws, customs, and usages of the tribe.

Senator SUTHERLAND. Do you mean to say that all those cases are cases of illegitimate children?

Mr CORNISH. No. I did not mean to say that. There are 1,500 of them.

Senator SUTHERLAND. Well, in the main?

Mr CORNISH. In the main, yes, sir.

Senator SUTHERLAND. I understood it to be asserted here yesterday—although perhaps I am mistaken about it—that at least prior to the passage of this law of 1888, or whenever it may have been, that in the Choctaw and Chickasaw tribes it was recognized that where a man and woman had lived together without anything more being shown—lived together in the habit of marriage, or lived together without the habit and repute of marriage—that that constituted a marriage under the rules and customs of the tribe.

Mr CORNISH. No, sir, that has not been stated by me.

Mr BALLINGER. Let us have that decision, please. When was it rendered, and by whom?

Senator LONG. As throwing some light on what was done in this case by the Commission, in this report of the Commissioner of Indian Affairs on the bill which is similar to this amendment, he says

This Office on December 26, 1906, wired the Commissioner of the Five Civilized Tribes as follows "Is it a fact that we enroll them as on the side of the father or mother?" to which the Acting Commissioner replied, under date of September 26. 1907: "Replying to your telegram 26th instant, tribal authorities of the Choctaw and Chickasaw nations in preparing tribal rolls enrolled children of Indian women by freedmen fathers as Indians. Tribal rolls clearly indicate that children of mixed freedmen and Indian descent follow status of mother."

Mr. CORNISH. There has never been, and can not be, any controversy about what the tribal custom was.

Senator BRANDEGEE. Let me ask you if the contention of Mr. Ballinger that the word ''descendants'' is synonymous with progeny. Then all the questions as to whether these claimants are legitimate or illegitimate, whether they knew their rights, or whether they thought they were compelled to make application for the assertion of those rights are irrelevant and immaterial, are they not?

Mr. CORNISH. Very largely, if not entirely so.

Senator McCUMBER. As I understand the general Indian custom is to recognize a woman outside of the tribe as belonging to the tribe when she marries a man in that tribe, and he remains. If he deserts his own tribe and goes to the tribe of the wife among the Indians, he becomes a member of the tribe to which the wife belongs. If that is the custom, it is more a question of which tribe they desire to remain in, but that ordinarily without a marriage of that kind the status of the child is always governed by the status of the mother.

Mr. CORNISH. Yes, sir.

Senator McCUMBER. But in the Choctaw and Chickasaw cases there was another special rule which arose by reason of their owning slaves, and which differentiated the case in this respect, that it did not recognize any child which was not one of regular marriage, where the mother was a slave, that it had to follow the status of the mother, even though it remained in and lived with the tribe.

Mr. CORNISH. Yes: the mother was in the enjoyment of a status of her own.

Senator McCUMBER. It was not a citizenship status?

Mr. CORNISH. No, sir; it was considered a citizenship; it conferred property and was considered a limited membership.

Senator BRANDEGEE. Do you know whether the Creeks owned any slaves?

Mr. CORNISH. Yes, sir; the condition in the Creek Nation differed entirely from the condition in the other nations. The Creeks, in their relations with their slaves, are entirely different. That has been explained to me in a very interesting way and I shall state it very briefly.

The Creeks occupied middle Alabama, and they had considerable trouble with the Government of the United States. A considerable portion of the Creeks and Seminoles are practically one tribe, and a considerable portion of them were driven out of Alabama and went into the Everglades of Florida. That was the place where every runaway negro went, and while the Creeks were inhabiting that part of the country, hiding from the pursuit of Andrew Johnson and his army, these runaways were there, and in that way those relations were established in those times, and thus the relations between the Creeks and the negroes with whom they associated took on an entirely different aspect from the relations existing between the other tribes and heir slaves—the Choctaws and Chickasaws and Cherokees.

The Cherokees resided in northern Georgia and the Choctaws and Chickasaws resided in central Mississippi; they owned their slaves, and when they emigrated they took their slaves along with them, and the relations there beginning and existing between the Choctaw an Chickasaw nations and their slaves parallel in all respects the relations existing between the white people and the slaves in other southern communities. They had much greater benefits, because since their freedom they have been permitted to occupy without restraint the land of the Choctaws and Chickasaws that they wished to cultivate.

Senator BRANDEGEE. I really had in my mind the question whether the Creeks, if they did own slaves in the South, took them to the Indian Territory?

Mr. CORNISH. Yes, sir; they took them to the Indian Territory, and I understand that there is a considerable portion of the citizenship of the Creek tribe where the blood is just as pure as it is in the Choctaw and Chickasaw nations; but the condition is said to account for the fact that a great many Creeks are mixed with negroes. They have accepted the negroes on a different footing from the rest of the tribes; but there can be no doubt on the proposition of the relations existing between the Choctaws and Chickasaws and their slaves.

Now, the difficulty of the whole matter is that these people are not willing to accept this. What they are asking is that they be given legislation which will be for their special benefit. It has been suggested that perhaps there is some desire on the part of the Choctaws and Chickasaws to contest their claims because of the fact that they are negroes. That is not true. Does it not appear, when we examine the treaties and laws from beginning to end, what their position is—not that it is the view of any of you gentlemen or any member of Congress, but it is their position that they should be given special rights and privileges because of their negro blood? These people come within the purview of this law which I have read, the act of May 31, 1900, which provides, in terms, that no man, woman, or child shall be enrolled unless his name appears on some one of the tribal rolls of the Choctaw and Chickasaw nations, or children born of that person since he came on the roll. There are before the Commission to the Five Civilized Tribes applications which have been made and are to-day being made which can not be considered upon their merits, of perhaps 20,000 persons from the States of Texas and Arkansas and other States. I am eliminating the great horde of persons who claim that they should be enrolled as Mississippi Choctaws. I have reference now to those persons who make no claims that they are Mississippi Choctaws.

There are thousands and thousands of persons who swear just as positively and as absolutely and will be able to submit evidence just as convincing as these people that they are of Indian blood, and they are barred by this law and by the act of July, 1902, because of the fact that the law which governs the jurisdiction of the Commission and the Secretary is that the customs and usages of the tribes as reflected in their tribal rolls is and must be observed, and those people are out. I am certainly not urging on you gentlemen that legislation be passed which would open up the whole subject again as to those 20,000 persons who are cut out by this law; but when I suggest that condition, when I suggest that those people are willing to swear just as positively and it will be just as difficult, if not impossible, for the tribes to meet their evidence as it would be to meet the evidence of these irresponsible people—when the condition exists as I have stated, would it seem to be quite fair, since their status is exactly what the status of the 20,000 persons is, to confer special benefits on those people because of the fact that they are possessed of negro blood, rather than discriminate against them because they are of negro blood?

So far as the law is concerned, so far as the power of the Government is concerned, so far as the jurisdiction of the tribunals of the Government is concerned, these 20,000 persons are out just as completely and they are out because of the provisions of the same law that applies to these people. I do not mean to say that if it should appear to you with absolute clearness and positiveness that these people were entitled to citizenship and rights, that it would be entirely fair and just to exclude them under a provision contained in the law. But I am endeavoring to convince you why there is no good reason that this should be done. We stand perfectly appalled at what may happen. It is almost beyond the power of the human mind to conceive what may result if what these gentlemen insist upon should be done. There is no way of meeting this evidence. It means, if you make it possible by opening this subject, for Mr. Campbell's opinion to be observed and applied to this condition, that every negro woman in the Choctaw and Chickasaw nations who is willing to swear that she had sexual intercourse, illicitly or otherwise, with some Indian man—and it is always an Indian now dead—and this particular child resulting from that union, according to the decision of Mr. Campbell, without reference to the laws or the customs of the tribe, without reference to all that, according to Mr. Campbell's opinion, that particular individual, on that evidence, will be entitled to be enrolled.

Now, there are from 1,000 to 1,500 of these persons, and it does not seem that their alleged rights have been suggested with sufficient strength and sufficient reasonableness to justify you in setting aside the laws or reversing the law of 1898, the decision of Mr. Vandevanter construing that law, the law of 1900, the law of 1902, and the law of 1906, and turning back the work of the Government for the past ten years and depriving the tribes of the safeguards that have grown up under their own customs, laws, and uses.

Now, gentlemen, I believe I am through. I may say that the subject is such a vast one; the proceedings have been so intricate that it is difficult at a glance, with the time you gentlemen have to devote to this proposition, to understand the various points at which applicants may gain an advantage, and the rights of the Choctaws and Chickasaws and the safeguards which have grown up may be beaten down.

Now, a provision could not be more objectionable than is contained in the proposed amendment—

That the Secretary of the Interior is hereby authorized and directed to transfer from the Choctaw and Chickasaw freedman rolls to the rolls of citizens by blood of said nations the name of any person who is of Indian blood or descent on either his or her mother's or father's side——

Now, at that point. That has never been suggested before. Mr. Ballinger is the pioneer following Mr. Campbell. Mr. Campbell is the real pioneer of the proposition that Indian blood alone conferred upon the person claiming Indian blood the right to participate in the tribal property. It has never been suggested by any person representing citizenship applicants before that blood alone—the establishment of some degree of Indian blood—was the only essential requisite to enrollment as an Indian and participation in the distribution of tribal property

Under the treaty of 1830 the tribal rolls were made up. They were made up first from the emigrant class who did those things which the Government of the United States required of Choctaw Indians under the treaty of 1830 that was that they were required to remove to and live upon the land of Choctaws and Chickasaws. The Choctaws and Chickasaws have followed that rule, but in the main their rolls have been made up first from that great class of persons who removed to and established their residence in the Choctaw and Chickasaw Nation, as the Government of the United States required them to do as one of the considerations upon which they acquired that vast area of land

Secondly the Indians that were the Mississippi Choctaws belonging to the class which remained behind them, from time to time came and were added to the tribal rolls. It was under those facts and these conditions and following those customs and usages that the tribes had made up their own tribal rolls. Now this states, following Mr Campbell. It says that the Secretary of the Interior may make —

Senator LONG. It directs him to

Mr CORNISH. Yes it directs him to transfer the name of any person who is of Indian blood. Now if you agree with that there is no way of describing what may happen. There are altogether 50,000 persons who are ready to swear and have sworn to furnish evidence of the fact whether it be good bad or indifferent

Senator SUTHERLAND. This resolution does not reach them

Mr CORNISH. Oh no these persons are situated, so far as their Indian blood is concerned, just as those other persons and the Commission and the Secretary of the Interior have followed the law very well. Mr Campbell has gotten off in a remarkable way, but I think we can find some way of preventing the threatened damage. But, in a general way they have followed the safeguards which Congress has put into the law and it could not possibly be opened wider than is proposed. The amendment says

The name of any person whose of Indian blood or descent on either his or her mothers or fathers side

Now that absolutely destroys with one stroke the customs and usages of the tribes which have grown up for generations

Senator LONG. That means either legitimate or illegitimate?

Mr CORNISH. Yes so

Senator LONG. Just so they have blood?

Mr CORNISH. Just so they have blood so they can establish it by any evidence they see fit to offer. As I say, that absolutely wipes out and destroys the protection which we have had under the customs and usages of the tribe, under which the tribal rolls were made, and which your tribunals must follow unless you see fit to change the law. The amendment continues

on either his or her mothers or fathers side as shown by either the tribal rolls the records prepared by and in the custody of the Commissioner to the Five Civilized Tribes or the Department of the Interior or by any governmental records in the possession of any Bureau Division or Commission or any of the Departments of the Government or any of the courts of the Indian Territory

Now, that provision has been drawn with some adroitness. They hope to impress you with the fact that they were not going to make use of the oral evidence, that they were not going to make use of these negro women who swear that they had sexual intercourse with the Indians. They sought to make the impression that the records were to be observed in drafting this, that they are not going to make any contention of that kind because they feel that that would not be permitted by Congress. So they say:

the records prepared by and in the custody of the Commissioner to the Five Civilized Tribes, etc.

The committee is perhaps not aware that immediately after the rendition of this decision by Mr. Campbell these thousand or fifteen hundred applications were made before the Commissioner to the Five Civilized Tribes, and the oral evidence of these mothers of these illegitimate children has already been taken, and is considered a part of the record of the Five Civilized Tribes, and they, under this provision, would have the benefit of that evidence. So that first the inference evidently was, or the intention was, in drafting this, to convince you that they were not going to open up the matter by oral evidence, but this would give them the benefit of all that ex parte evidence. That can not be met. If it is permitted that an irresponsible negro woman—I do not say she is irresponsible because she is a negro—but if an irresponsible negro woman gives oral evidence that five years ago she had sexual intercourse with a particular Indian man who is dead, how can the tribes meet that? It can not be met; it is impossible.

Gentlemen, I stand appalled at what may result, and I really think the possibility of permitting a condition of that character will perhaps appall you gentlemen. I do not believe you are going to do it.

Senator WARNER. Were you present to cross-examine these witnesses as attorney for the Indians?

Mr. CORNISH. We had a representative present in a great many instances. [Reading on:]

and persons having rights conferred by this act shall be entitled to establish only by evidence their descent from persons of Indian blood and recognize the members of the tribes as appears from any such record.

Now, that would not only permit them to make use of all this oral evidence which has been taken before the Commission, but it would absolutely deprive us of the benefit of the tribal rolls, so far as the fixing of the status of the father is concerned. They not only wish to be permitted to make use of this evidence, which has been taken under the circumstances I have described, as fixing the circumstances under which the child was begotten, but they wish not to be bound by the rolls in fixing the status of the alleged progenitor. [Reading on:]

and persons having rights conferred by this act shall be entitled to establish only by evidence their descent from persons of Indian blood and recognized members of the tribe as appears from any such record. *Provided further*, That nothing herein shall be construed so as to permit the filing of any original application for the enrollment of any person not heretofore, and at the time of the passage of this act, enrolled as a freedman of either the Choctaw or Chickasaw Nation, or who has an undetermined application for such enrollment now pending, it being the purpose of this act to provide only for a correction of the enrollment of persons of Choctaw or Chickasaw Indian blood who have been enrolled as freedmen of said Nations——

Why not permit those people from Texas and other States? There are 20,000 of them. They swear just as strongly, and in so far as the evidence is concerned, it is just as good as this evidence. Why keep them off? They swear that they have the blood; they have the right.

They moved into the Choctaw Nation. Now they are cut off just as these people are——

and no limitation of time in which to file original applications, or to perfect appeals, heretofore fixed by law, shall be construed as a bar to rights conferred by this act; and any person so transferred may contest any allotment heretofore made to which he or she had a superior right at the time of his or her erroneous enrollment, provided, however, that such contest shall be instituted within ninety days from the date of such transfer and that patent has not issued from such allotment.

Senator LONG. What does that mean—"has a superior right"?

Mr. CORNISH. The right of possession, I suppose. For instance, here is a particular person who had particular land. He is entitled to that to the extent of 40 acres. But that would permit him to make out more.

Senator LONG. To make out an Indian allotment?

Mr. CORNISH. Yes, sir.

Senator LONG. Also that has been allotted to some other Indian; is that what that means?

Mr. CORNISH. I think it does: yes, sir.

Senator McCUMBER. Did not a great many of these freedmen settle and live on land outside of their 40 acres?

Mr. CORNISH. Oh, yes; they occupied vastly more than 40 acres.

Senator McCUMBER. And would that not refer to the land which they occupied outside of the 40 acres?

Mr. CORNISH. Very likely. I think that means to say that if they were in possession of more land than the 40 acres they are now confined to that.

I have consumed a good deal of time on this subject; this is about all I have done since 1898, and if there is any further information that I can give I will be glad to do so.

Senator LONG. How many freedmen are there on the rolls of the Choctaw and Chickasaw nations?

Mr. CORNISH. Between 10,000 and 11,000 on those two rolls; a little over 5,000 Chickasaws and a little less than 6,000 Choctaws.

Senator DUBOIS. How many Choctaw and Chickasaw Indians?

Mr. CORNISH. Between 25,000 and 30,000 on both rolls.

Senator McCUMBER. Have you filed a brief in this case?

Mr. CORNISH. I submitted my views at McAlester before the select committee, and they have been transcribed.

Senator McCUMBER. You submitted an oral argument?

Mr. CORNISH. Yes, sir; which was taken down and has been transcribed.

Senator McCUMBER. This is simply a repetition of that, is it?

Mr. CORNISH. Yes, sir; but this is more in detail than the statements I made before the select committee.

Senator McCUMBER. I can see, so far as I am individually concerned—without passing on the question—that this amendment is broad enough undoubtedly to admit to citizenship on the evidence which could be secured of everyone who had Indian blood or who could say they had Indian blood; they could probably all get on the rolls under it. So that would bring it right back to this question, whether or not under the customs of the tribe they would be entitled to become citizens under their customs or their laws; and if they were entitled I should not object to their all going on, even though it would discriminate to a great extent. We get right back after all to the real question, not whether they have been guilty of laches, but whether or not they are entitled under the laws and customs to be regarded as citizens of that community. I presume you have something more definite, or at least as fully definite as this, upon that subject.

Mr. CORNISH. This is really the statement I wish the committee to consider. As to that particular point, I have said that the tribunals of the Government of the United States, for the purpose of making up the citizenship rolls and for the purpose of dividing the property; that the limit of the Government's jurisdiction is the tribal rolls themselves, which were made by the tribes in pursuance of their customs and laws. There is no power anywhere to add a single name to any roll. The final tribal roll must be the tribal roll of the tribe; the final roll made by the Government must be the roll of the tribe, and children born to those persons since those rolls were made, and intermarried persons, less such persons as may be eliminated from the tribal rolls because placed thereon without authority of law.

Senator McCUMBER. Suppose we did pass a law of that kind and should find that that law was harsh; that it did exclude those who ought to have been in justice placed on the rolls, you would not object to our still allowing them to be placed on the rolls, provided we were satisfied that they were really entitled under the customs of the tribe to be placed there?

Mr. CORNISH. Of course I could not take issue upon that question. I am compelled to assume that Congress, whatever it does, is doing what it thinks is right, and if Congress should feel that those persons, or any other persons, are really entitled to go on those rolls and entitled to land, I could expect you to do it.

Senator BRANDEGEE. But of course it is your duty as an attorney to protest against it.

Mr. CORNISH. No, sir; it is not. I want to say a word as to that. Our instructions from the tribe have been not only to prevent the enrollment of those persons not entitled, but to give substantial assistance to those who are; to make the road easy; to make the proper construction of the law. We have agreed to a construction of all those laws which we think is just and correct. Now, our instructions from the beginning are not only to protest against those persons not entitled, but to devote our time and efforts and the means of the tribe to the assistance of those persons who are entitled.

Senator BRANDEGEE. But I understood you to say before our subcommittee out there, time and again, whenever you got a chance, that you did not want any more people put on these rolls, but that the matter should be regarded as closed.

Mr. CORNISH. I said that as the existing law now stands the matter will be closed.

Senator BRANDEGEE. I say it is your duty now as their attorney to protest against any other persons being put on.

Mr. CORNISH. Yes, sir; to protest. But no injustice will be done to anybody; all persons will be on under the existing law, and the law will take its course.

Senator LONG. After ten years in trying to perfect these rolls they feel that all persons who have any right to be on the rolls are there now.

Mr. CORNISH. Yes, sir; and a great many more. Gentlemen, I thank you for your attention.

ADDITIONAL STATEMENT OF MR WEBSTER BALLINGER.

The CHAIRMAN Mr Ballinger, do you desire to reply?

Mr BALLINGER I shall be very brief I desire in the commencement of my remarks to refer to the decision of the Indian Office

Senator SUTHERLAND Is it the same letter that you read before?

Mr BALLINGER Yes, sir In the decision of the Commissioner of June 14, 1906, denying the petition for the transfer of the name of Calvin Newberry et al from the roll of Chickasaw freedmen to the roll of citizens by blood of the Chickasaw Nation, he held

It does not appear from the records of this Office that any application was made for the enrollment of the petitioners or any of them as citizens by blood of the Chickasaw Nation prior to December 25, 1902

The Commissioner of Indian Affairs, in bringing this case to the attention of the Secretary of the Interior in a communication which also included his recommendation that the decision of the Commissioner be affirmed, says

The Commissioner finds that the Department in its letter says that in view of the fact that the records of his Office are under the provisions of the act of Congress approved April 26, 1906 (34 Stat L 137), conclusive as to these applications, and further search should be made of the records for the purpose of ascertaining if any application was made by the persons named in Mr Lee's affidavit for citizenship in the Chickasaw Nation under the provisions of the act of June 10, 1896 The Commissioner reports * * * that there was filed with the Commission on September 9, 1896 a petition of Callie Newberry praying for admission to citizenship in the Chickasaw Nation

* * * * * * *

He reports that the original petition in the case is not in the possession of his Office, and it is not believed to be probable that it is now in existence but he does find from the records of his Office that from the adverse decision rendered by the Commission on November 10, 1896 an appeal was taken to the United States court for the southern district of the Indian Territory

The Commissioner further says that notice of this appeal was furnished the Commission * * * and it was directed that all the original papers be immediately forwarded to the court to be used and considered in the case of Callie Newberry et al v The Chickasaw Nation

* * * The Commissioner says that Mr Lee now seeks to invoke the aid of the records of the United States court for the purpose of showing that such an application was made under the act of June 10, 1896

The Commissioner quotes from section 4 of the act of Congress approved April 26, 1906 supra as follows That no name shall be transferred from the approved roll of freedmen or any other approved rolls of the Choctaw Chickasaw Cherokee Creek or Seminole tribes respectively to the roll of citizens by blood unless the records in charge of the Commissioner to the Five Civilized Tribes show that application for enrollment as a citizen by blood was made within the time prescribed by law by or for the party seeking the transfer and such records shall become conclusive evidence as to the fact of such application unless it be shown by documentary evidence that the Commission to the Five Civilized Tribes actually received such application within the time prescribed by law and says that provision of the act in his opinion prohibits the transfer of names of persons from the approved rolls of Choctaw and Chickasaw freedmen to the rolls of citizens by blood of the Choctaw and Chickasaw nations unless application * * * was made on or before December 24, 1902, * * * and that the copy of the affidavit of Callie Newberry of August 31 1906 can not in any manner be construed as an application for citizenship of her seven children * * * but admitting that this affidavit * * * is construed as an application submitted on behalf of these persons he is of opinion that they would be bound by the decision of the Commission of November 10, 1896, denying the petition filed by Callie Newberry on September 10, 1896

Mr Bixby holds that the petitions submitted on behalf of Choctaw and Chickasaw freedmen for admission to citizenship in the Choctaw and Chickasaw nations under the act of Congress approved June 10 1896 and which were denied can not as held by the Department in its letter of May 25, 1906 (I T D 9114 1906) be construed as continuing applications as contemplated by section 4 of the act of Congress approved April 26, 1906

The letter of the Department of date of May 25, 1906, herein cited by the Commissioner, and which is used by the Commissioner for the purpose of defeating the rights of all persons not defeated by section 4 of the act of April 26, 1906, and which upsets all the decisions of the legal officers of the Department, as well as the decisions of the Attorney-General, was written by a lunatic, insane at the time he prepared the letter, later adjudged to be crazy by the supreme court of the District of Columbia, and by its decree incarcerated in St. Elizabeth's Insane Asylum.

Senator BRANDEGEE. Who is that communication signed by?

Mr. BALLINGER. It is signed by Mr. C. F. Larabee, Acting Commissioner of Indian Affairs.

Mr. CORNISH. I think it would be worth the committee's while to get at a disposition of this matter. How do the papers in that case differ from the papers which were discovered in the Joe and Dillard Perry case?

Mr. BALLINGER. In the Joe and Dillard Perry case they had never been transmitted to a court—the case had never been before a court—but on the contrary had been actually in the possession of the Commission at all times. There is no question in the world but that the Perry application, at the time of the certification of the record to the Department, was in the possession of the Commission, and was suppressed for the sole purpose of defeating their rights to enrollment as citizens by blood.

Mr. CORNISH. Do I understand you now that the physical paper, which you say has the virtue of an application, is now in the physical possession of the Commission?

Mr. BALLINGER. No; of record with the court.

Mr. CORNISH. All the records of the United States court were sent to the Choctaw and Chickasaw citizenship court, and were, by order of the Department, turned over to the Five Civilized Tribes, and are now in their files.

Mr. BALLINGER. They were in all cases in which the Choctaw and Chickasaw citizenship court assumed jurisdiction, but that court did not assume jurisdiction of either the Perry or the Newberry case.

Mr. CORNISH. Then why did you not go to the United States court and get a certified copy of this paper?

Mr. BALLINGER. The Commissioner sent to the court and got the original papers and a copy of the docket entries in this case in conformity with departmental instructions, and transmitted them to the Department with the request that they be returned to him in order that they might be returned to the court.

Mr. CORNISH. That is the original paper in that Newberry case, which you say has the virtue of an original application; that is the application.

Mr. BALLINGER. The application is on file with the court.

Mr. CORNISH. Now, why did you not go to the court and get a certified copy of it and file it with the committee?

The CHAIRMAN. I think that why he does not do a thing is not proper.

Senator LONG. I think it is very proper that you bring it out because in a letter to the select committee under date of November 24, 1906, Mr. Bixby says:

Since the passage of this act no cases have been determined by this office wherein it was necessary to a decision in the case upon just what constitutes "documentary evidence,' as used in section 1 but as illustrative of the character of the examination had in these cases there is attached hereto (marked Exhibit J") the examination had on May 28 1906 in the matter of the application for the enrollment of Joshua Willie and Frank Impson as citizens by blood of the Choctaw Nation In this case a statement is made in the record or notations which appear upon the freed card upon which these children were listed when application was originally made for their enrollment before the Commission in 1899

Reference is also made to certain notations found on Choctaw roll card, field No. 1829 upon which card appears the name of Morris Impson the alleged father of these children

Then he goes on and says:

I think I can safely state that every facility has been afforded applicants enrolled as freedmen of the Choctaw and Chickasaw nations and who now desire to be enrolled as citizens by blood of one of said tribes to show by any evidence in the possession of this office whether a notation upon our field card letters in the files of this office, or testimony or other evidence on file in the case under consideration or other cases that an application was made or attempted to be made for their enrollment as citizens by blood prior to December 25 1902, the time limited for the reception of such applications by the act of July 1, 1902

Mr BALLINGER My associate, Mr Lee, calls my attention to the fact that his sworn statement as to precisely what the record contains is in the record, if you remember, of the hearing before the committee.

Senator LONG Is it a certified copy of the record or the record itself? His affidavit might not be considered documentary evidence

Senator BRANDEGEE But Mr Bixby himself or one of his employees there, in the hearing that was had before us, I remember, testified to certain things that he had construed as being applications, and when that——

Senator WARNER But it is said in this extract that he held it was not a continuing application

Senator BRANDEGEE He gave instances of certain things that he decided to be documentary evidence

Mr CORNISH Yes, now, it won't do for Mr Ballinger to say——

Mr BALLINGER I mean to say that either in that paper right there or the decision in the case—and I have in my possession all the papers in the case where it is stated that the papers were transmitted to the Commission by the court and by the Commission certified to the Department and that they were considered by the Department that is, the Indian Office—and then returned

Mr CORNISH A certified copy of the papers?

Mr BALLINGER The original papers

Mr CORNISH There is some mistake about that

Senator BRANDEGEE Well, there is no use in disputing that until we get the papers

Mr BALLINGER By permission of the committee, I will print the full communication of the Commissioner of Indian Affairs to the Secretary, in which he sets out the decision of the Commissioner and recommends that the decision of the Commissioner be affirmed, and the decision of the Secretary affirming it, to appear at the conclusion of my remarks I desire, if I can, to make very clear to whom this grant was made It has been contended here that it was made to the Choctaw Nation and that the Choctaw Nation could control its own citizenship, that it could put on the rolls such persons as it saw fit, and that by so doing confer upon them property rights, that it could strike from those rolls the names of such persons as it saw fit, and likewise deprive them of property rights In short, that the nation alone could determine its membership, and thus determine the property rights of all persons under the treaty of 1830.

Let us analyze the language used in the treaty and made the operative words of grant in the patent. The grant was:

To the Choctaw Nation, in fee simple to them and their descendants, to inure to them while they shall exist as a nation and live on it.

The grant was not limited exclusively to the nation as then existing, but was exclusively limited to the then existing community of Choctaw Indians and to their descendants in fee simple, to inure to them. To whom did it inure? To them, the descendants of those persons then comprising the community of Choctaw Indians, which community constituted the nation. What does the word "inure" mean, and for what purpose is it here employed? It means: 1, "to pass into use; 2, to take or have effect; 3, to serve to the use or benefit of." (Bouvier and Universal Dictionary.)

And it was employed for the purpose of passing the communal estate to the descendants of the then community of Choctaw Indians to serve to the use or benefit of them.

Now, let us rewrite this section and insert in lieu of the word "inure" these words of definition.

The grant would then read:

To the Choctaw Nation, in fee simple to them and their descendants, to pass into use for them while they shall exist as a nation and live on it.

Or

To the Choctaw Nation, in fee simple to them and their descendants, to take or have effect as to them while they shall exist as a nation and live on it.

Or

To the Choctaw Nation, in fee simple to them and their descendants, to serve to the use or benefit of them while they shall exist as a nation and live on it.

The word "descendant" meaning:

A person who is descended from another; anyone who proceeds from the body of another, however remotely.

And the word "inure" meaning: 1 "to take or have effect as to them; 2, to pass into use for them; 3, to serve to the use or benefit of them."

We thus determine beyond question the true meaning and intent of this language.

Again, the word "descendant" is not employed in legal phraseology as a technical word used in connection with governments for the purpose of defining their natural acts and powers.

Nowhere in legal phraseology is the word "descendant" one of the technical legal words employed in a grant to vest in the now existing individual absolute indefeasible title. The accepted universal technical legal words employed being: "heirs," "successors," and "assigns."

The word "descendant" not being one of the accepted technical legal words employed in vesting title in fee simple in a now existing person, it must be construed in accordance with its true meaning and given the full import of that meaning.

Thus the word "descendant" here is used for the sole purpose of fixing the rights in a communal estate of persons yet unborn whose rights in such estate attach simultaneously with their birth and become vested.

"Where a treaty admits of two constructions, one restrictive as to the rights that may be claimed under it and the other liberal, the latter is to be preferred (Shanks v. Dupont, 3 Pet., 242). Such is the settled rule of this court," so said Mr. Justice Swayne in delivering the opinion of the court in the case of Hauenstein v. Lynham, 100 U. S., 487, and citing the above-referred-to decision by Mr. Justice Story.

This being the settled rule of the Supreme Court of the United States, certainly a reasonably liberal construction of the word "descendant" would include not only the children but the grandchildren and the great grandchildren, and so on to the remotest degree, even though the more remote descendants were not possessed of as great a quantom of Indian blood as the ancestor.

Nor could it have been the intention of the contracting parties that only legitimate issue, as technically defined and recognized in civilized communities, should take under the grant.

The people comprising the Choctaw Nation in 1830 were living in a state of nature. The mere living together of a man and woman constituted a valid marriage. The abandonment of the wife by the husband constituted a valid divorce, and the issue of such unions were possessed of all their natural rights. (Robertson's History of America, Book 4; Wall v. Williamson, 11 Alabama, 839; Johnson v. Johnson, Administrator, 9 Mo. Reports, p. 88.)

The rule prevailing at the time the treaty was signed must continue to the time of the distribution of the property. You can not have one rule for one period of time and another for another period of time. You must construe the treaty of 1830 according to the intention and understanding of the contracting parties at the time it was negotiated. The rule prevailing at the time the treaty was negotiated must continue to the time of the distribution of the property, and you can not turn aside into the genealogy of individuals or be turned aside by the peculiarities of Indian laws and customs.

To permit the Indian tribe to determine who were its members and who were entitled to participate in the distribution of the tribal property would be to commit individual rights to the incompetent and corrupt hands of those who have a direct pecuniary interest in the decision.

As the tribal lands in Indian Territory were ceded to the Choctaw Nation in consideration of the cession by the Choctaws of lands east of the Mississippi, not even Congress could divest any persons entitled to share in the tribal lands under and by virtue of the treaty of 1830. In the case of Jones v. Meehan, 175 U. S., p. 1, Mr. Justice Gray, in delivering the opinion of the court, said:

The construction of treaties is the peculiar province of the judiciary, and except in cases purely political Congress has no constitutional power to settle the rights under a treaty or to affect titles already granted by the treaty itself. (Wilson v. Wall, 6 Wall., 83, 89, 18 L. ed., 727–729; Reichart v. Felps, 6 Wall., 160, 18 L. ed., 849; Smith v. Stephens, 10 Wall., 321, 327, 19 L. ed., 933, 935; Holden v. Joy, 17 Wall., 211, 247, 21 L. ed., 523, 535.)

In the case of Wilson v. Wall (6 Wall., 83), hereinabove cited, the power of Congress to affect the property rights and titles of Choctaw Indians secured to them by the treaty of 1830, the identical treaty under which the petitioners herein claim property rights, is determined. In passing upon the effect of an act of Congress enacted for the purpose of ascertaining the names of parties entitled to patents under the treaty of 1830 and the quantity of land to which each was entitled, the court says:

It (the act of Congress) can not affect titles before given by the Government, nor does it pretend to do so. Congress has no constitutional power to settle the rights under treaties, except in cases purely political. * * * The legislature may prescribe to the Executive how any mere administrative act shall be performed, and such was the only aim and purpose of this act.

Now let us see whether or not that was the interpretation of the treaty of 1830, as construed by the parties themselves as late as 1866, and whether or not these nations were vested with power by the treaty of 1830 to adopt people into the tribe with full communal property rights.

Article 26 of the treaty of 1866 provides:

The right here given to the Choctaws and the Chickasaws, respectively, shall extend to all persons who have become citizens by adoption, or intermarried with either of said nations, or who may hereafter become such.

Article 38 provides—and this is an important article:

Every white person who, having married a Choctaw or Chickasaw and resides in the said Choctaw or Chickasaw nation, or who has been adopted by the legislative authorities, is to be deemed a member of said nation, and shall be subject to the laws of the Choctaw and Chickasaw nations according to his domocile, and to prosecution and trial before their tribunal, and to punishment according to their laws, in all respects as though he was a native Choctaw or Chickasaw.

Senator McCumber. That excludes color by including white?

Mr. Ballinger. Article 3 provided for the adoption, after the nation had adopted laws, rules, and regulations, of those persons then living and formerly held in servitude, and their descendants.

Senator McCumber. Adoption, but not with full rights in the nation.

Mr. Ballinger. All the rights, privileges, and immunities of any other citizen, except the right to take property equally with the others, and gave them 40 acres of land.

Senator McCumber. That would be a complete right of a citizen, would it not?

Mr. Ballinger. Yes, sir; with a limited property right. Article 26 conferred all rights given by an article of the treaty upon all persons who might become citizens of the tribes by adoption and intermarriage, while article 38 conferred equal rights with Choctaws and Chickasaws upon white persons intermarrying or adopted into the tribes. Until this treaty of 1866 was ratified, however, no person whomsoever theretofore adopted by the tribes or who had intermarried into the tribes had secured by his adoption or intermarriage a right to participate in the communal lands or other property of the tribes, and neither of the parties to the contract of 1830 believed that the tribes could confer those rights, as is clearly indicated by these articles.

Then, again, article 45 provides:

All the rights, privileges, and immunities heretofore possessed by said nations, or individuals thereof, or to which they were entitled under the treaties and legislation heretofore made and had in connection with them——

What legislation? Congressional legislation.

shall be, and are hereby, declared to be in full force, so far as they are consistent with the provisions of this treaty.

The rights conferred by the treaty of 1830 upon the descendants of the then Choctaws are reaffirmed by this treaty article

But let us see what the powers of the Choctaw and Chickasaw nations or the powers of any Indian government are to divest a person of a right given such person under a treaty

Senator McCumber You claim that the Indian nation had no power to divest descendants of any kind of a right—unborn descendants?

Mr Ballinger No, sir, it had not as long as the property was held by the community under the unchanged terms of the treaty of 1830

Senator McCumber Suppose an Indian tribe had ceased to exist as a tribe and had become dispersed or scattered over the country and ceased to hold its tribal property, would not the land under this grant revert to the Government?

Mr Ballinger Undoubtedly it would

Senator McCumber Then they could by that act deprive the descendant of a right granted under the act?

Mr Ballinger In that case the nation and its people would have by their own act forfeited their property, for the treaty of 1830 provided that the land should revert to the Government in the event the nation ceased to exist as a nation and live on it The object sought by the treaty was this It was to place that title in some name that would live and pass on down through generations in order that the children and their children and their children might take property rights as they were born, that was the object

Senator McCumber The only reason I asked the question was probably to demonstrate what was in my mind—that if the tribe could by its own act dissolve itself as a tribe entirely destroy its tribal relations, then certainly it must also convey the power to restrict its citizenship If it can destroy its citizenship, it would certainly have the lesser power to restrict its citizenship and determine who should be members and who should not

Mr Ballinger But it would be for the United States Government and not the tribe to determine and declare the forfeiture Let us suppose one case of restriction and regulation of membership by the tribe, if that be true, and those were the powers of that nation; let us suppose that the nation adopted an equal number of white people into the nation, that portion of the white people thus adopted secured control of the political affairs of the nation, they could then, under that theory, divest all those of Indian blood of their citizenship and the grant would inure to the white people

Senator McCumber No, that would not follow They could enact a law by which certain others— marriages outside of their tribe, for instance— should not become citizens They could prevent this from occurring any more by making restrictive rules, but they could not deprive one existing at that time of the right

Mr Ballinger I have a clear-cut blanket decision on that point It is the case of the New York Indians where the grant was made to the confederated tribes They attempted to limit descent to the mother, and provided that wherever a male member of the tribe married a white woman, outside of the tribe, that the children of such union should take the status of the white woman and not become members That was a law of the nation That case was recently adjudicated by the Court of Claims, having been referred there by act of Congress, and the Court of Claims, when it came to render its opinion in that case, decided all these questions and brushed them aside as though they were of no consequence, and issued a decree directing the distribution of tribal property to all persons who were parties to the treaty or whose ancestors were, without regard to restrictive tribal laws or questions of blood and citizenship.

Senator WARNER. You quote that decision, do you not?

Mr. BALLINGER. No, sir; I do not. I tried to get the decision last night, but I was unable to, and with permission I will insert it in my remarks.

Senator CLARK, of Wyoming. How long ago was that made?

Mr. BALLINGER. That decision was rendered, I think, on the 15th day of May, 1905.

Senator BRANDEGEE. Suppose you get the titles of those cases and file them.

Mr. BALLINGER. Very well, I will insert the decision. I find this in a Cherokee case, where the Cherokees adopted under treaty with the Government the Delaware Indians, and I find that the Cherokee Nation attempted to exclude the Delaware Indians from participation in their tribal property.

Senator CLARK, of Wyoming. Did not that case grow up on the terms of a contract whereby the Delawares paid a certain amount of money for what land they should occupy and for citizenship in the tribes?

Mr. BALLINGER. Yes, sir; and under the terms of the treaty providing for it, and the Cherokee Nation sought to divest the Delawares of their property rights.

Senator CLARK, of Wyoming. Did not that arise on a contract between the two peoples—the Delawares and the Cherokees—that is the question I asked.

Mr. BALLINGER. Yes, sir; I think it did.

Senator BRANDEGEE. The syllabus will show.

Mr. BALLINGER. Yes, sir; I will read the syllabus. It is on page 199, volume 155, United States Supreme Court Reports. The Cherokee Nation v. Journeycake.

Senator LONG. It construed the agreement or treaty?

Senator CLARK, of Wyoming. There was a treaty made and those two tribes entered into a definite contract.

Mr. BALLINGER. The right of the contract turning upon the right of a native Cherokee under the treaty, it is pertinent to inquire what the rights of the native Cherokees were under the treaty and as to whether or not the Cherokee Nation could divest a native Cherokee.

Now, the distribution of the property was about to be made under an agreement with the Government; it has only been a few years ago that this decision was rendered. The court says, on page 216:

It is also worthy of note that when in 1883 a bill passed the national council for the payment to the native Cherokees alone of a certain sum of money received as rental from the Cherokee Strip Live Stock Association, which, so far as appears, was the first manifestation of a claim of a difference between the native Cherokees and the registered Delawares as to the extent of their interests in the lands or the proceeds thereof, it was vetoed by D. W. Bushyhead, the then principal chief of the Cherokee Nation, on the ground that such action was in violation of the agreement of 1867. It is true the bill was passed over his veto. While the veto message is too long to quote in full, these extracts sufficiently disclose the reasons upon which it is based:

Third. The "patent" was made to the "Cherokee Nation" in 1838, and the Cherokee Nation was then composed of citizens by right of blood, and so continued to be until the exigencies of the late war arose, when, in 1866, it became necessary to make a new treaty with the United States Government. By this treaty, made by and with this nation, other classes of persons were provided to be vested with all the rights of "native Cherokees" upon specified conditions. These conditions have been fulfilled as regards the acknowledged colored citizens of this nation and the so-called Delaware and Shawnee citizens. I refer you to article ninth of said treaty in regard to colored citizens, and article fifteenth, first clause, as regards Indians provided to be settled east of 96°. The language is, they shall have all the rights of native Cherokees "and" they shall be incorporated into and ever after remain a part of the Cherokee Nation on equal terms in every respect with native Cherokees.

Sixth. If the lands of the nation were and are the common property of citizens, then no citizen can be deprived of his or her right and interest in the property without doing an injustice and without a violation of the constitution which we are equally bound to observe and defend. While the lands remain common property, all citizens have an equal right to the use of it. When any of the land is sold under provisions of treaty, all citizens have an equal right to the proceeds of their joint property, whether divided per capita or invested.

"Senators, such is the treaty and such is the constitution. I have referred you to them and stated their evident meaning in the premises "to the best of my ability," as is my duty. To the classes of citizens this bill would exclude, attach "all the rights and privileges of citizenship according to the Constitution." To three of these classes attach also the rights of "native Cherokees," according to treaty."

Further comment on this case is unnecessary. We see no error in the conclusions of the Court of Claims, and its decree is affirmed.

Counsel for the Choctaw and Chickasaw nations seems to concur in our construction of the treaty of 1830, viz, that under that treaty the word "descendant" was used for the sole purpose of fixing the rights in a communal estate of persons yet unborn whose rights in such estate attach simultaneously with their birth and become vested.

He also admits that the Chickasaws were adopted into the Choctaw Nation under and by virtue of the treaty of 1837, and that the property right acquired by the Chickasaws was "to be held on the same terms that the Choctaws now hold it." What were the terms upon which the Choctaws held it? The terms of the treaty of 1830 which ceded the lands—

to the Choctaw Nation, in fee simple, to them and their descendants, to inure to them while they shall exist as a nation and live on it.

Mark you, the grant here was not to the Choctaw Nation as then existing, or as it existed at any future time, but was exclusively limited to the then existing community of Choctaw Indians and to "their descendants," in fee simple, to inure to them. Under this grant, the terms of which were embodied in the patent, and the patent has never been changed, no person could acquire property rights in the Choctaw Nation unless he was a recognized member of the community which constituted the Choctaw Nation at the date of the negotiation of the treaty of 1830, or unless the ancestors of such person were recognized members of that community.

TREATY OF 1855.

The treaty of 1855 has been referred to in this discussion for the sole purpose of confusing the real issues. It does not in any way impair the rights given persons by the treaty of 1830 granting the lands to the Choctaw Nation. Nor has any court or any legal officer of the Government, or anyone else possessed of legal knowledge, except the attorney for the Choctaw Nation, ever contended that this treaty changed the terms of the grant made under the treaty of 1830. No new patent has ever been issued and in the patent are the identical words contained in the treaty of 1830:

The United States, under a grant specially to be made by the President of the United States, shall cause to be conveyed to the Choctw Nation a tract of country west of the Mississippi River, in fee simple, to them and their "descendants," to inure to them while they shall exist as a nation and live on it.

The object sought to be accomplished by the treaty of 1855 was set out fully in the preamble, as follows:

Whereas the political connection heretofore existing between the Choctaw and the Chickasaw tribes of Indians has given rise to unhappy and injurious dissensions and controversies among them which render necessary a readjustment of their relations to each other and to the United States; and

Whereas the United States desire that the Choctaw Indians shall relinquish all claim to any territory west of the one hundredth degree of west longitude, and also to make provision for the permanent settlement within the Choctaw country of the Wichita and certain other tribes or bands of Indians, for which purpose the Choctaws and Chickasaws are willing to lease, on reasonable terms, to the United States that portion of their common territory which is west of the ninety-eighth degree of west longitude; and

Whereas the Choctaws contend, that by a just and fair construction of the treaty of September 27, 1830, they are of right entitled to the net proceeds of the lands ceded by them to the United States under said treaty, and have proposed that the question of their right to same, together with the whole subject-matter of their unsettled claims, whether national or individual against the United States arising under the various provisions of said treaty, shall be referred to the Senate of the United States for final adjudication and adjustment; and whereas it is necessary for the simplification and better understanding of the relations between the United States and the Choctaw Indians that all their subsisting treaty stipulations be embodied in one comprehensive instrument:

Now, therefore, the United States of America, by their Commissioner, George W. Manypenny the Choctaws, by their commissioners. Peter P. Pitchlynn, Israel Folsom, Samuel Garland, and Dickson W. Lewis, and the Chickasaws, by their commissioners, Edmund Pickens and Sampson Folsom do hereby agree and stipulate as follows, viz.

The above preamble recites the precise objects sought to be attained, and states that as the Choctaw and Chickasaw people were having serious contentions as to their separate national political rights, the distribution of the funds derived from the sale of the lands formerly held and occupied by the Choctaws and situated east of the Mississippi River, and as the United States Government desired to locate certain tribes or bands of Indians, including the Wichitas, on the tribal lands lying west of the one hundredth degree of west longitude, and commonly known as the Lease District, and to induce the Choctaws to relinquish all right thereto and to secure a release from the Choctaws and Chickasaws of that portion of their common territory west of the ninety-eighth degree of west longitude, "this treaty is negotiated."

Article 1 of the treaty provides as follows:

ARTICLE 1. The following shall constitute and remain the boundaries of the Choctaw and Chickasaw country, viz: * * *

And pursuant to an act of Congress, approved May 28, 1830, the United States do hereby forever secure and guarantee the lands embraced within the said limits to the members of the Choctaw and Chickasaw tribes, their heirs and successors, to be held in common, so that each and every member of either tribe shall have an equal, undivided interest in the whole. Provided, however, that no part thereof shall ever be sold without the consent of both tribes, and that said land shall revert to the United States if said Indians and their heirs become extinct or abandon the same.

The term "heirs" as applied to the communal estate of the Choctaws and Chickasaws is a misnomer.

Bear in mind that the individual members of the Choctaw and Chickasaw nations had merely a life interest in the usufruct of the land conveyed by the patent of 1842, which patent was issued under and by virtue of the treaty of 1830, and that the fee never became absolute in the individual, but remained in the communities or nations so long as they should exist as nations, and the persons comprising the nations should continue to live on the land. The Indians' estate was therefore a communal estate. The fee was lodged in the Choctaw Nation for the benefit of the descendants of those persons comprising the Choctaw Nation, subject, however, to the condition that if the nation ceased to exist as a nation and its members ceased to occupy and live on the land the land should revert to the United States.

Therefore the word "heirs" could have no legal significance, as the nations then had no laws governing "descent and distribution," and as no definition of the word "heirs" can be found in the treaty the word can only be construed under the common law. The American and English Encyclopedia of Law, in defining the word "heir," says—

At common law, an heir is he who is born or begotten in lawful wedlock, and upon whom the law casts an estate in lands, tenements, and hereditaments immediately upon the death of the ancestor.

Could the death of an ancestor "cast an estate" in communal lands upon his heirs, then members of said nations, who acquired full right to participate in the tribal property by birth? As the ancestor acquired only a life interest in the usufruct of the land, and as that right terminated with his demise, he never had an interest in the communal lands possible of being transmitted to his heirs. He enjoyed the fruits of his birthright during his life and his rights in the communal lands terminated instantaneously with his demise and passed back to the community. In the case of Brown v. Belmarde (3 Kans., 41) the court defines the right of the individual member both before and after the vesting in him of an individual title. The court said—

Prior to the treaty of 1825 the Kansas Nation of Indians had the Indian title to the land in controversy, i.e., the right to use, occupy, and enjoy. This title was by the sixth article vested in Laventure. His title was no greater than that of the nation had been. The nation's title was transferred to and invested in him individually. After the boundaries were ascertained in the manner contemplated in the treaty, he was the sole owner of section 9 to the extent of the Indian title. His interest did not amount to an estate of inheritance, but was a mere life interest in the usufruct. There are no words in the treaty which, upon any known rule of interpretation, would create an estate of inheritance. Before the treaty the United States held the ultimate title with the right of undisturbed occupancy and perpetual possession in the Indian nations so long as it should remain a nation. Had the nation become extinct without a treaty the lands would have become the property of the United States disencumbered of Indian title. So after the treaty Laventure having but a life estate to the extent of the Indian title in section 9 should he die with or without issue the whole title to that section would vest in the United States.

As the word "heirs" as used, when construed under the common law, can have no legal meaning, we must naturally look to the substance of the treaty to ascertain, if possible, the intention of the contracting parties and to give to it that construction the parties thereto intended it should have.

Article 7 of said treaty guarantees to the members of said nation—

The unrestricted right of self-government and full jurisdiction over persons and property within their respective limits, excepting, however, all persons or members who are not by birth, adoption, or otherwise citizens or members of either the Choctaw or Chickasaw tribe, and all persons not being citizens or members of either tribe shall be considered intruders and be removed from the same by the United States agent.

Citizenship in said nations sprang from, i. e., (1) birth and (2) adoption as declared by this article. The right to participate in tribal property, lands, moneys, or otherwise, and to all privileges and immunities exercised or enjoyed by any other member of said nations or tribes, attached to the individual immediately on his birth, which was simultaneous with his citizenship in said nations.

In the light of article 7, hereinabove quoted, is it possible that the contracting parties intended to use the word "heirs" in the legal or ordinary acceptation of the term? We insist that they did not, and that the attempt here made by counsel for the nations to so construe renders the word utterly meaningless. The term "heirs"could have legal meaning only when used in connection with "lands, tenements, and hereditaments," which by operation of law descend on the death of the person legally seized in fee to such persons as are by law declared to be his heirs. No individual citizen of said tribes was seized in fee of tribal lands; therefore, the word "heirs,"as herein used, is devoid of legal meaning or significance.

In the case of McGuire v. Moore (108 Mo., 267), the court said, in construing a will:

> It is proper where the face of the whole will, or of the particular clauses, relating to a certain subject warrant, and justice and reason require it, that the word "heirs" may be construed as "children" or "issue," "grandchildren" or "descendants." (Waddell v. Waddell, 99 Mo., 345; Chew v. Keller, 100 Mo., 369.)

The court further said:

> Expounding the will in this way is certainly in accord with the intent of the testator, as explained by himself, and this expounding results in saying that the word "heirs" must mean children of the former or of the then present husband.

Following the decision of the court hereinabove cited, counsel for petitioners insist that the word "heirs" should be construed as though it were "descendants," as used in the treaty of 1830, as such a construction only will give to it any legal significance and at the same time carry out the intention of the contracting parties.

A descendant as defined by the Encyclopedia of Law and Procedure, volume 13, page 1047, is—

> One who descends, as offspring, however remotely; correlative to ancestor or an ascendant; one who has issued from an individual, including children, grandchildren, and their children to the remotest degree.

In Van Buren v. Dash (30 N. Y., 393), per Denio, C. J., the court defines "descendant:"

> Thus we speak of the descendants of Abraham, of William the Conqueror, of George the Third, and of the first and second President Adams, of Jefferson, and Alexander Hamilton, while we say of Queen Elizabeth, of William of Orange, of Washington, and Madison, that they left no descendants, or, in the words of the statute, that they, respectively, died, leaving no child or other descendant. These are common forms of speech, and the meaning is perfectly definite, and it is such as I have mentioned. The word is invariably employed in that sense in books of history, in memoirs, in biographies, in works of genealogy, and in most every book which treats of men and their affairs.

Following the established meaning of the word "descendant" as it has come down to us from time immemorial through decisions of the highest courts of England and this country and as defined by all authorities, the Assistant Attorney-General of the United States for the Department of the Interior, in the case of Joe and Dillard Perry, under date of February 21, 1905 (see opinions Attorney-General,

1905), in passing upon a case involving rights similar to the rights of your petitioners, thus defines it

'Descendants as pointed out in the case of James W Shirley is a term of wider significance than heirs' or 'legitimate issue,' and includes those springing from an ancestor whether legitimate issue or not

CITIZENSHIP AS DEFINED BY THE ASSISTANT ATTORNEY-GENERAL OF THE UNITED STATES

The word "heirs," as used in the treaty of 1855, does not and can not affect the rights of your petitioners to full citizenship in said nations. Certainly the child of a recognized member of either of said tribes born in lawful wedlock, according to the laws, usages, and customs of said tribes prevailing at the date of the treaty of 1830, and born in the nation, having continued residence therein and owing his allegiance thereto, is a citizen of the nation He derived his allegiance of birth by succession to the allegiance of the parent His rights were clearly defined in the case of Mary Elizabeth Martin, decided by the Assistant Attorney-General for the Department of the Interior and approved by the Secretary on March 24, 1905 In said opinion the Assistant Attorney-General says

Allegiance of birth is obtained by succession to the allegiance of the parent This is the fundamental and universal law of all organized societies or States and essential to their continued existence as such

In no State, so far as I am aware, has it ever been held that the offspring of a citizen is a born stranger to the parents' allegiance, outcast from the parents' civil state, citizen of no other, merely because the parent was born to, and for some part of its life owed, a foreign allegiance It is not the parents' race or blood that gives citizenship to the child, but the parents' status of citizenship at the child's birth

If the status of an adopted citizen, having no Indian blood and previously owing his allegiance to a foreign government deriving his right to citizenship solely by adoption, entitles his child to the father's tribal status, how can it be denied that the child of a citizen by blood of the Choctaw Nation, always resident therein and having owed his allegiance to no other government, did not take his status of citizenship in said nation at the time of his birth and by reason of his father's blood and status as a member of said nation

INTENTION OF CONTRACTING PARTIES TO TREATY OF 1855

When we consider the treaty of 1855 in its entirety, we are irresistably impelled to the conclusion that the contracting parties intended to use the word "descendants" instead of the word "heirs" The second paragraph of article one unqualifiedly secures to the members of the said nations all the guarantees contained in the treaty of 1830 relative to the lands conveyed said nation under the latter treaty The treaty of 1830 was to "the Choctaw Nation and their descendants" So also article seven defines "citizens or members" of said nations to be persons resident within said nations who derived or acquired a tribal status by reason of "birth, adoption, or otherwise" This would seem to be conclusive as to the intention of the contracting parties to adhere strictly to the terms of the treaty of 1830 and the patent issued thereunder The treaty of 1855 was not negotiated with a view to changing or altering the terms of the original grant, but to make them more secure to the people of the Chickasaw Nation in common with the people of the Choctaw Nation under the grant.

Following the thus established meaning of the word "descendant" as it was understood by the contracting parties to the treaty of 1830, when the Choctaws were living in a state of nature, Congress in enacting laws and ratifying agreements for the dissolution of the tribal government and the allotment of the lands of the Indians in severalty, has used the identical word used in the treaty of 1830—"descendants." The word appears in the act approved June 7, 1897, which act construed and defined the words "Rolls of citizenship" used in the act approved June 10, 1896. So also the word "descendants" is used in the act approved June 28, 1898, under which these people were enrolled, and in subsequent acts.

No court in the land, and no judicial officer of the Government, and no other individual, except the attorney for the Choctaw Nation, has ever even advanced the idea that the treaty of 1855 fixed the rights of any person to participate in the tribal lands of the Choctaw and Chickasaw nations, or in the remotest degree interfered with or affected rights conferred by the treaty of 1830.

Senator McCUMBER. Putting to you an extreme case, do you hold that if an Indian of this tribe—Choctaws or Chickasaws—should marry a married Indian—say he has a family—should marry there and go over to Mexico and live there two or three years, and have children by a Mexican woman, would those children be entitled to rights in the tribe? Of course that is an extreme case.

Mr. BALLINGER. I will answer your question, and answer it frankly. I do not believe that when they leave their tribal community and go elsewhere that their rights continue.

Senator McCUMBER. No; that is not it. Suppose he goes over there, but does not intend to desert his tribe, lives there a while and has children and comes back into his tribe and lives there recognized as a member, would those children of a Mexican mother, in a foreign country, be members of the tribe?

Mr. BALLINGER. If he returned, the citizenship of the children would be his citizenship, and his citizenship being that of the Chickasaw, their citizenship would be that of the Chickasaw, and undoubtedly, in my opinion, the rights would be fixed as such.

Senator McCUMBER. Suppose he did not bring his children with him at all, but returned himself, would the children become citizens?

Mr. BALLINGER. Such a condition as that is impossible in this case, because the law provides that they must return, and that they must be residents when they were examined, and when these rolls were made in 1898.

Senator McCUMBER. That is the question of putting them on the rolls, but you are to put citizens only on those rolls. The question is whether those would be citizens and entitled to go on the rolls.

Mr. BALLINGER. If they did not return they could not go on, because the law expressly excludes them.

Senator McCUMBER. Suppose they came back and made application?

Mr. BALLINGER. If they returned—

Senator McCUMBER. Now, the children returned—perhaps it is not proper to use that expression—but suppose the father returned and brought back his illegitimate children?

Mr. BALLINGER. If he abandoned his citizenship in the nation and went off to Japan or somewhere else and there acquired another citizenship——

Senator McCUMBER. That is not the proposition that I make. I say that he does not abandon his citizenship.

Mr. BALLINGER. Then their citizenship is his, and that is fixed, and they would be members of that tribe.

Senator McCUMBER. Now, just one step further. He is declared by the laws of the United States to be a citizen of the United States. Would the children thereby become citizens of the United States, and if he brought back this woman, she of course would not be his wife if he was married, but suppose he was not, and he brought back this other woman, would she thereby become a citizen of the United States?

Mr. BALLINGER. She would be a citizen of the United States with a right to take in the tribal property.

Senator McCUMBER. Yes; a citizen of the United States because all the members of the tribe are declared to be citizens of the United States.

Mr. BALLINGER. In the first place, in order to take under these laws she must have, since a recent date, married in conformity with tribal laws. If she did not marry in conformity with the tribal laws she would be barred under the holding of the Department. But in my judgment if she returned with him to the nation and lived in the United States she would be entitled, providing the question of marriage is settled. Her children certainly were, and I am not sure but what she was.

Senator LONG. Suppose an Indian, a Chickasaw, had a Chickasaw wife and three children by her, and had two children illegitimately with a freed woman, would the children of the freed woman be descendants and entitled?

Mr. BALLINGER. Unquestionably, under both of the decisions of the Department, and in my opinion under a proper construction of that grant, and I do not see how you can get away from it, as they would be a part of the community.

Senator BRANDEGEE. Would a citizenship depend on legitimacy?

Mr. BALLINGER. No, sir.

Senator BRANDEGEE. Suppose a child was born on an ocean steamer of an Indian who was on a trip, would he not be a citizen if his father was a citizen?

Mr. BALLINGER. Certainly he would.

Senator STONE. Do you mean an illegitimate child?

Senator BRANDEGEE. Is not an illegitimate child a citizen of the United States in that case; do they not follow the status of their father?

Mr. BALLINGER. I made the statement yesterday that if a natural child was begotten by an Indian man on a white woman, and she not a citizen of this nation, that that child would take, as a citizen of the nation, an allotment, and would be enrolled.

Senator LONG. Whether there was marriage or not?

Mr. BALLINGER. Whether there was any marriage or not, and regardless of whether the father was married at the time the child was begotten.

S. Doc. 257, 59-2——7

Now I am going to read from an opinion of the Choctaw and Chickasaw citizenship court, and I want to ask the attorneys for the nations if they know of or have ever heard of a decision of the Department or the courts which is contrary to this decision. I read from page 167 of the compilation by the Department of the last decisions and regulations affecting the work of the Commission:

Taking this to be true, then, if there was no marriage the children of Lucy were illegitimate, begotten by a full-blood Choctaw Indian. This court has held in a case (Althea Paul et al. v. Choctaw and Chickasaw nations) that when there was a natural child begotten by a Chickasaw Indian on a white woman the child was entitled to enrollment as a member of the tribe by reason of the Chickasaw blood of his father.

That is the court that knocked off, I do not know how many thousand people. That is what the court says, and if the Department or the courts in these cases has or have ever varied from that holding I now invite correction of my statement.

That is the decision of the Choctaw and Chickasaw citizenship court referred to in the decision of the Department. Now, I want to inquire if that is true with reference to a child begotten by an Indian man on a white woman. Is it to be reversed with reference to the child begotten by an Indian man on a negro woman? The same general principle must apply.

It has been stated here repeatedly that there are many negro persons of negro blood on those rolls. I have purposely hesitated about referring to those. There are 200 negroes without one drop of Indian blood in their veins on the rolls of the Choctaw Nation. Have you ever attempted to strike those names from that roll? Those names were placed there by the act of the council of 1896. They were adopted by the Choctaw Nation, for what purpose I am not now going to discuss, but those people were adopted and their names placed on the tribal roll, and unless I am mistaken—and if I am I invite correction—they are to-day on the tribal rolls prepared by the Commission and have received their allotments.

Mr. CORNISH. You invited interruption. What is your statement now?

Mr. BALLINGER. My statement is that under the instructions given by the Choctaw Nation in 1896—and I had them here yesterday—200 negroes without one drop of Indian blood in their veins were placed on the Choctaw rolls.

Mr. CORNISH. That is just as untrue as it can be. It is absurd.

Mr. BALLINGER. The instructions directed the names to be placed upon the rolls.

Mr. CORNISH. The freedmen in the Choctaw and Chickasaw nations have been adopted as freedmen; the freedmen are enrolled and adopted as freedmen, but the statement that 200 persons have been enrolled as citizens is absurd.

Mr. BALLINGER. Those people that I have referred to have not one drop of Indian blood in their veins.

Mr. CORNISH. That statement I unequivocally deny, and I hope the committee will not give consideration to your bare statement contradicted by mine, unless you have evidence to support it.

Mr. BALLINGER. I will furnish those instructions.

Mr. CORNISH. What instructions?

Mr. BALLINGER. The instructions that were given by the Choctaw legislature to the committee that prepared the roll in 1896 and directed the enrollment. The first instruction was to enroll every person of Choctaw blood born and raised in the Choctaw Nation. That was the first instruction given by that legislature.

Mr. CORNISH. What next?

Mr. BALLINGER. I do not recall them; but that was the first instruction, to enroll every person of Choctaw blood born and raised in the Choctaw Nation.

Mr. CORNISH. And they did so?

Mr. BALLINGER. They did not enroll those people. Now, it has been said—

Mr. CORNISH. If you will pardon me, you invite contradiction, and if it is disagreeable to the committee I shall not contradict you. Now, I want to state—

Mr. BALLINGER. Any statement that I make here I invite contradiction and correction of.

Mr. CORNISH. You make the statement and I deny it; now, what proof have you?

The CHAIRMAN. If you have the proof present it; if not, file it later.

Senator WARNER. You have not those instructions here, have you?

Mr. BALLINGER. I have them in my papers and I will supply them and put them in my remarks.

Senator McCUMBER. I can not understand what they will prove. Suppose you grant the power of the tribe to increase its members and to adopt citizens, what does that do?

Mr. BALLINGER. Mr. Cornish says there has been no discrimination against the negro. I say that there has been by certain chiefs and certain headmen and certain officials down there, that those names were put on the tribal rolls, and I reassert that.

Senator WARNER. It was favoritism in making up the rolls.

Mr. BALLINGER. Here is the act of the Choctaw legislature approved October 10, 1896.

ACT OF CHOCTAW LEGISLATURE APPROVED OCTOBER 30, 1896.

*   *   *   *   *   *   *

SEC. 3. *Be it further enacted:* It is hereby declared the duty of the Commissioners to examine the rolls made by the Commission appointed under the act of September 18th, 1896, and also to expunge from said rolls of September 18th, 1896, the names of all persons whom they shall adjudge not to be citizens; and also to expunge from the rolls of freedmen and the leased district rolls all such names adjudged not to be citizens, the intention being that the name of no person adjudged by these Commissioners a non-citizen shall appear on any rolls as a citizen. The Commission shall enroll as citizens all who come under any one of the following heads, and all such persons are hereby declared to be citizens of the Choctaw Nation:

I. All Choctaws by blood born and raised in the Choctaw Nation.

II. All Choctaws by blood who have been admitted to citizenship by the general council and now residents of the nation.

III. All white men who married Choctaw women before the treaty of 1866 in accordance with the laws of the Choctaw Nation.

IV. All white men who have married Choctaw women by blood in accordance with the Choctaw laws of 1866 and the law of 1875 relating to intermarriage, and have not been divorced from them and have maintained a bona fide residence in the Choctaw or Chickasaw Nation.

V. All white men who have married Choctaw women by blood in strict conformity with the laws of the Choctaw Nation of 1875 regulating intermarriage, or the Choctaw law of 1876 regulating intermarriage, and have not been divorced from same nor married any other than a Choctaw woman by blood since said marriage.

VI. All negroes who were enrolled and declared to be citizens of the Choctaw Nation by the registration board of 1883.

VII. All descendants of such enrolled negro citizens since registration.

VIII. All white women who have married Choctaws by blood legally, and who have not been divorced from them or since married any other than a Choctaw by blood, a recognized citizen and resident of the Choctaw or Chickasaw Nation.

IX. All Choctaws by blood who are now serving terms in the penitentiary who, at the time of their conviction and sentence, were residents of the Choctaw or Chickasaw Nation.

And the Commission are especially prohibited from enrolling as citizens any persons coming under the following heads:

I. Negroes, noncitizens, who have intermarried with negro citizens.

II. The children of any marriage where neither the father nor mother are Choctaws by blood, though one or both of said children's parents may have enjoyed intermarriage rights.

III. All persons who, though they had at one time intermarried rights, afterwards married a person not a Choctaw by blood (being the father or mother of Choctaw citizens shall not save a person from this clause).

IV. All white men who took Choctaw women by blood and went without the jurisdiction of the Choctaw Nation and were there married.

V. All white men who married Choctaw women by blood in the Choctaw Nation, but not according to Choctaw law.

VI. All persons who have been admitted to citizenship with their wife or husband by the general council and afterwards the wife or husband, Choctaw by blood, dying, the surviving party, being a white person, has intermarried with a person not a Choctaw by blood.

VII. All persons who have applied for citizenship and have not been accepted by the general council.

VIII. All persons born out of wedlock, except the mother be a Choctaw by blood: *Provided,* The children of negro women and their descendants, registered as citizens by the board of freedmen registration, though born out of wedlock, shall be registered.

I reassert that in the preparation of the tribal rolls by the Commission they did not adhere to the tribal rolls. I assert, in the case of Boss McCoy—and the evidence is in that record, in the form of certified copies—that Boss McCoy's wife's name appeared upon the roll of 1885 and that the names of each one of his children born prior to the preparation of that roll were on that roll, and I assert that each and every one of those children have been enrolled as freedmen by the Commissioner and his decision approved by the Secretary. There is a tribal recognition; they did follow it in that case, and they have not followed it in but very few cases.

Now, it said that if you open these rolls the padding of them will be beyond comprehension; it will be appalling. Senators, we ask in this case that you give these people the rights which they had under the law under which they appeared before the Commission in 1898. If the Commission at that time had inserted in the record the words "application for enrollment as a citizen," we would not be here before you to-day. That is all there is lacking in any one of these cases—those three or four words, "application for enrollment as a citizen." If those words had been placed in these records, these people would have been enrolled and would be on the citizenship rolls to-day. Mr. Cornish asserts that the Perry decision enunciates a new doctrine, a new idea. The members of the committees—freedmen committees and others, who sat with this Commission in the Indian Territory—and I am asserting now that which is in the record and that which is sworn to by a man, for whose integrity Mr. Cornish vouches, who says that they appealed to his committee for enrollment as citizens; that he was instructed by the Commission to deny them their rights and to report their cases only for enrollment as citizens.

That is the question. It is not a question now as to whether or not they took allotments as freedmen. The question is, Were they given that kind of enrollment under the act under which they appeared before the Commission? And if they had not appeared, the Commission could have summoned them, it had all the power it was possible to give a Commission to bring them in arbitrarily; and when they brought them in, it was directed by the Assistant Attorney-General, in the very decision that was referred to, to enroll them as citizens if the names of their ancestors appeared on any tribal rolls "The act of 1897 did not provide for new applications for citizenship neither did the act of 1898 make any provisions for new applications for citizenship" That is what Attorney-General Van Devanter said to the Commission when it was proceeding under the act of 1898, and notwithstanding those instructions, prepared by an admittedly great jurist, the Commission asserts now that it was necessary for them to make an application That is all there is lacking in this case—an application for citizenship

Now, it is said that Attorney-General Van Devanter in his decision held that these people were not entitled to enrollment I am going to show you by this decision that he held that they were entitled to enrollment Here is what he said

They were not authorized to add any name not found upon some roll of the tribe except those of descendants of persons rightfully upon some roll and persons intermarried with members of the tribes and therefore lawfully entitled to enrollment

These people are descendants—descendants within every possible meaning of the word They were directed to enroll them and they did not do it

Senator McCUMBER They were descendants of those on the roll?

Mr BALLINGER Yes, sir

The CHAIRMAN Please read that again I do not think it is limited to any roll

Mr BALLINGER Here is the language

They were not authorized to add any names not found upon some roll of the tribe, except those of descendants of persons rightfully upon some roll and persons intermarried with members of the tribes and therefore lawfully entitled to enrollment

That included these people and their descendants It is stated that the Commission has enrolled all persons rightfully entitled to enrollment under the tribal laws That I deny, and I assert now and here that the Commission never has had in its possession all of the tribal rolls of these nations It had in its possession certain rolls, and it has selected which one of those rolls it would use as a basis I deny that the rolls that it has in its possession are correct rolls Why? Because those rolls were made up from county rolls in the Choctaw Nation, and the Commission and the nation in making the one roll did not place upon the one roll all the names that were on the county rolls Now, those county rolls were certainly as correct as the rolls selected by the Commission to be used by it as a basis of determining who were entitled to enrollment and who were not Some of those rolls are in the Treasury Department—tribal rolls upon which moneys have been paid to people down there

They have never been in the possession of the Commission, the Commission knows not whose names are on those rolls, and yet they say that these people are not entitled to enrollment because their names are not on the rolls selected by them as their standard The Commission gives sanctity to some rolls and casts all other tribal rolls out as spurious General Van Devanter—and he is one of the ablest men who ever presided over that Department—held that if they were descendants of persons whose names were on any tribal rolls, they were entitled to enrollment. That is all we are contending for.

Now, there have been many other things dragged into this controversy; it has ramified all over all classes of cases. Now, the facts in connection with the Mary and Elizabeth Martin case were not correctly stated. I will state them, and if my statement is not absolutely correct I invite interruption. The case of Mary and Elizabeth Martin was this: The father of that girl intermarried into the Choctaw Nation; the mother of that girl intermarried in the Choctaw Nation, and both were adopted and became citizens. The Indian husband of the adopted white woman died, and the Indian wife of the adopted white man died, and the widower and widow, both adopted into the nation, intermarried.

Senator CLARK, of Wyoming. Both white?

Mr. BALLINGER. Both white. But both of them intermarried citizens of the nations, and the contention was that the child of the two citizens was a citizen, and it is a natural and logical contention, for certainly the child takes the citizenship of one parent or the other, and it could not take the citizenship of either without becoming a citizen of the nations. Am I correct in that statement, Mr. Cornish?

Mr. CORNISH. That is substantially correct, but it has no bearing here. In referring to the Martin case, you said yesterday that that decision of Mr. Van Devanter's in that case was the law at this time and never had been overruled.

Senator LONG. Mr. Campbell recited that.

Mr. CORNISH. Yes, sir.

Senator McCUMBER. What was the decision in that case?

Mr. BALLINGER. That the child was entitled to enrollment. That was not only Mr. Campbell's decision in that case, but Judge Clayton's decision in similar cases in the Territory, and the books are full of similar decisions.

Senator LONG. It was the Attorney-General's decision?

Mr. BALLINGER. I think it was argued and reargued and submitted and resubmitted to the Attorney-General's Office. It was then after having been reaffirmed by the Assistant Attorney-General, that it was referred to the Department of Justice. I have never seen the decision of the Attorney-General in the case, but I understand that he made a memorandum statement that the child was not entitled to enrollment, and that statement has been lodged somewhere—either sent here to the Capitol or lodged in the Department of the Interior, and that case is now before the Attorney-General for consideration.

The CHAIRMAN. I think it was a letter; I think we had it here last winter in connection with this discussion.

Senator McCUMBER. What did he hold?

The CHAIRMAN. He reversed Judge Campbell, as I recall it.

Mr. BALLINGER. I do not know anything about that, but I do not want the committee to lose sight of the fact that both of these people were citizens. During this discussion there has been a great ramification over court decisions, and it has been said that if you open up these rolls as prepared by the Commission you are going to bring in twenty or fifty thousand people who are as much entitled to enrollment as these people. That I deny. They may have Indian blood in them, but they left the nation and went off into Texas and other States and did not return to the Indian Territory and appear before the Commission and ask for consideration in 1898. They never were entitled to it under the law, because they were not citizens and residents of the Indian Territory; they were not, in fact, citizens of the nations, and therefore their application, if they made one, was, and must necessarily be, denied. These people were born in the nation and their parents enrolled; their fathers are enrolled, and they are denied the citizenship of their father. They have been born and raised in his home; he was a citizen; they grew to man's estate and participated in elections. Their citizenship has never been questioned or denied in the Choctaw Nation. The chief justice of the Choctaw Nation, in the Buckholts case, which I referred to yesterday, held that the citizenship of the father carried with it the citizenship of his descendants. I mean that the recognition of the father as a citizen by blood carried with it the recognition of his descendants; that is the language.

Now, if there is anything that can bind the Choctaw Nation it is the decision of it's own courts—the highest court in the nation—and that is what their supreme court asserts to be the law. Here is an exact copy of what is in the book. I read from page 109. In the opinion of the Assistant Attorney-General for the Department of the Interior in the case of James M. Buckholts, it is stated:

William Buckholts applied under this act to the supreme judges of the Choctaw Nation to have his citizenship rights determined; that the said William Buckholts attempted to include the names of his descendants in his application, but was informed by the chief justice that this was unnecessary and that his (William Buckholt's) recognition as a Choctaw by blood carried with it the recognition of his children——

Senator McCUMBER. His children by whom?

Mr. BALLINGER. It does not say; the facts do not appear in the decision as reported.

Senator LONG. That is important.

Mr. BALLINGER. It proceeds:

That for this reason, and following the general custom in such cases at that time, the names of his descendants were not included in said application.

Mr. CORNISH. The Senator makes an inquiry, and I think I can furnish the information. These are very well-known people in the Choctaw and Chickasaw nations. There can be no question of their legitimacy. They are well-to-do people there. I am stating that as a matter of general information.

Mr. BALLINGER. If that be true why was it that in this decision the word "descendants" was used? Why did it not say his legitimate children and grandchildren? But it says "descendants," in exact line with the treaty of 1830.

Senator BRANDEGEE. What does he say--recognition of what?

Mr. BALLINGER. Recognition of his descendants as citizens.

Senator SUTHERLAND. He uses both words there, his children and afterwards he uses the word "descendants" as practically synonmous.

Senator BRANDEGEE. Do these people vote there? Are your claimants voters there?

Mr. BALLINGER. They have participated in every tribal election. Is that not true?

Mr. CORNISH. No; that is not true. In the Choctaw Nation the Choctaw freedmen have been adopted and have participated in the tribal elections, but the Chickasaws have never given any recognition to their freedmen until the law of 1898, when provision was made for tentative allotments of 40 acres.

Senator McCUMBER. The treaty gives them the right to take part in the voting, etc.?

Mr. CORNISH. If they shall have been adopted in accordance with the treaty. The treaty of 1866 gives the Choctaws and Chickasaws the right to adopt; the Chickasaws never did adopt them, but the Choctaw freedmen do participate in the election.

Mr. BALLINGER. Here are the constitutional requirements. Let us see whether these people are eligible or not to hold any office from principal chief down.

Senator DUBOIS. It is with regard to the Chickasaws that he makes the point.

Mr. BALLINGER. Let us see about it in the Chickasaw Nation. The Chickasaw constitution provides that:

Article 2, section 3.—All free persons of the age of 19 years and upward, who are by birth or adoption members of the Chickasaw tribe of Indians and not otherwise disqualified, and who shall have resided six months immediately next preceding any election in the Chickasaw Nation, shall be deemed qualified electors under the authority of this constitution.

Article 4, section 3.—No person shall be a representative unless he be a Chickasaw by birth or adoption * * *.

Article 5, section 3.—No person shall be eligible to the office of governor unless he shall have attained the age of 30 years and shall have been a resident of the nation for one year next preceding his election. Neither shall any person except a Chickasaw by birth or an adopted member of the tribe, at the time of the adoption of this constitution be eligible to the office of governor.

Senator LONG. Does that include freedmen?

Mr. BALLINGER. It includes descendants by birth in the nation; persons of Indian blood born in the United States.

Senator McCUMBER. Read that again.

Mr. BALLINGER:

Article 2, section 3.—All free persons of the age of 19 years and upward, who are by birth or adoption members of the Chickasaw tribe of Indians and not otherwise disqualified, and who shall have resided six months immediately next preceding any election in the Chickasaw Nation, shall be deemed qualified electors under the authority of this constitution.

Article 4, section 3.—No person shall be a representative unless he be a Chickasaw by birth or adoption * * *.

Article 5, section 3.—No person shall be eligible to the office of governor unless he shall have attained the age of 30 years and shall have been a resident of the nation for one year next preceding his election. Neither shall any person except a Chickasaw by birth or an adopted member of the tribe at the time of the adoption of this constitution be eligible to the office of governor.

Senator McCUMBER. They have to be a member of the tribe by birth or adoption?

Mr. BALLINGER. Certainly; the birth in the nation of a child to a citizen carries with it the citizenship of the parent. From where could a child get his citizenship except citizenship by birth or adoption?

Senator LA FOLLETTE. Does that make them members of the tribe?

Mr. BALLINGER. Certainly it does; he is a qualified elector there and a man capable of holding any office under the tribe.

Senator STONE. As a matter of fact do they exercise it?

Mr. Cornish. No; they do not. They never have.

Mr. Lee. If you will allow me to make a statement, I will give as a concrete case this Newberry case that has just been quoted. A senator of the Chickasaw legislature stated under oath, and his affidavit will be offered in this case, that those Newberry boys appeared at an election to vote; a question was raised as to whether they were entitled to vote, and, that certain old well-known citizens of the nation and officers of that election determined that they were entitled to vote and were citizens of the nation; and this senator goes further and states that he considered that the vote of these men elected him a senator of the nation.

The affidavit is as follows:

AFFIDAVIT OF JAMES A. ALEXANDER.

Indian Territory, *southern district, ss:*

James A. Alexander, first being duly sworn, on his oath states that he is 43 years of age, a resident of the city of Ardmore, Chickasaw Nation, Indian Territory; that he was born and raised in the Indian Territory. Deponent states that his grandmother on his mother's side, who died about eight years ago at the age of 90, was a Love and the aunt of one Ben Love. Deponent states that he has often heard his grandmother say that Caldonia Newberry was the daughter of Ben Love, a Chickasaw Indian of about seven-eighths blood.

Deponent further states that at an Indian election held at Rock Springs in the year 1890 he was a candidate for election to the Indian senate at which election the Newberry boys, sons of the said Caldonia Newberry, who appeared to cast their votes, were questioned as to their right to do so, whereupon deponent's uncle, Frank Colbert, stated to the judges that the Newberrys were descendants of Ben Love and a mixed breed woman, and were entitled to vote in said election; that it was so ordered and they did vote, electing deponent to the senate.

Further, deponent says that the Caldonia Newberry above referred to, who is making this application, is the same as has been pointed out to him all his life by his grandmother as the daughter of the said Ben Love.

                                        James Arthur Alexander.

Subscribed and sworn to before me this 22d day of June, 1905.

[seal.]   J. McNaught,
        Notary Public for the Southern District, Indian Territory.

Senator Warner. And the Newberry boys were what?

Mr. Lee. They were that class of persons—mixed Indian and negro—who are now enrolled as freedmen by the Commission.

Mr. Cornish. There may be an isolated case of that kind.

Mr. Ballinger. This is no isolated case. The rule applied in all cases, and I assert from the record in this case that these people have been citizens and are citizens to-day. Mr. Chairman, owing to the fact that it is getting late, and I think nearly every phase of this question has been covered, except the decision in the case of the New York Indians *v.* The United States, which is as follows, I will close, thanking you for your courteous consideration.

The CHAIRMAN. As I understand, this amendment is a tentative proposition. If the committee should decide to go into that matter they will take up the question of the details.

The committee thereupon adjourned.

---

*DECISION OF THE COMMISSIONER AS SET OUT IN THE DECISIONS OF THE COMMIS-
SIONER OF INDIAN AFFAIRS AND THE DEPARTMENT, AND THE DECISIONS OF
THE COMMISSIONER OF INDIAN AFFAIRS AND THE DEPARTMENT IN THE NEW-
BERRY CASE.*

DEPARTMENT OF THE INTERIOR,
OFFICE OF INDIAN AFFAIRS,
Washington, December 3, 1906.

The Honorable the SECRETARY OF THE INTERIOR.

SIR: I have the honor to invite your attention to the inclosed letter of September 17, 1906, from Tams Bixby, Commissioner to the Five Civilized Tribes, who acknowledges the receipt of Departmental letter of July 14, 1906 (I. T. D. 8093–1906), inclosing for consideration and report a communication of June 20, 1906, from Albert J. Lee, an attorney at law of Ardmore, Ind. T., relative to the petition of Calvin Newberry et al. for the transfer of their names from the roll of Chickasaw freedmen to the roll of citizens by blood of the Chickasaw Nation.

The Commissioner says that Mr. Lee inclosed with his letter a copy of the order or decision of the Commissioner of June 14, 1906, denying the petition for the transfer of the names of Calvin Newberry and his minor children, Ethel and Mabelle Newberry; Simon Newberry and his minor children, Isom, Bertha, Ben, Lillie, and Mary Newberry; Willie Newberry and his minor children, Effie, Wiley, Willie, and Sadie Newberry; Louis Newberry and his minor child, Lula Newberry; Mira Stevenson and her minor child, Grady Stevenson; Lula Stevenson and her minor child, Loan Stevenson, from the roll of Chickasaw freedmen to the roll of citizens by blood of the Chickasaw Nation.

The Commissioner further says that Mr. Lee also transmits his affidavit of June 20, 1906, wherein he alleges that the docket of citizenship cases in the office of the clerk of the United States court for the southern district of the Indian Territory at Ardmore, having record of the cases appealed from decisions of the Commission to the Five Civilized Tribes under the act of Congress approved June 10, 1906 (29 Stat. L., 321), shows that the application was made on August 31, 1896, by Callie Newberry for the enrollment of herself and Sam, Willie, Louis, Calvin, Mariah, Lula, and Lydia Newberry for citizenship in the Chickasaw Nation, to the Commission to the Five Civilized Tribes under the act mentioned above.

The Commissioner finds that the Department in its letter says that in view of the fact that the records of his office are, under the provisions of the act of Congress approved April 26, 1906 (34 Stat. L., 137), conclusive as to these applications, and further search should be made of the records for the purpose of ascertaining if any application was made by the persons named in Mr. Lee's affidavit for citizenship in the Chickasaw Nation under the provisions of the act of June 10, 1906.

The Commissioner reports that in his decision or order of June 14, 1906, denying the petition for the transfer of the names of Calvin Newberry et al. from the roll of Chickasaw freedmen to the roll of citizens by blood of the Chickasaw Nation, it was held that—

"It does not appear from the records of this Office that any application was made for the enrollment of the petitioners or any of them as citizens by blood of the Chickasaw Nation prior to December 25, 1902,"

and that he finds from an examination of the records of the Commission to the Five Civilized Tribes, in reference to applications submitted under the provisions of the act of June 10, 1906, that there was filed with the Commission on September 9, 1896, a petition of Callie Newberry praying for admission to citizenship in the Chickasaw Nation.

This petition was docketed as "1896 Chickasaw citizenship case No. 111," and he says it appears to have been considered and adjudicated by the Commission on November 10, 1896, when an order was entered denying the petition.

He further finds that this case appears on the 1896 citizenship docket of the Commission now in his office as follows:

111 Callie Newberry v Chickasaw Nation Elmore Ind T

Filed September 9 1896 Answer filed
Application denied "

He reports that the original petition in the case is not in the possession of his office, and it is not believed to be probable that it is now in existence, but he does find from the records in his office that from the adverse decision rendered by the Commission on November 10 1896 an appeal was taken to the United States court for the southern district of the Indian Territory

The Commissioner further says that notice of this appeal was furnished the Commission to the Five Civilized Tribes by the clerk of the United States court for the southern district of the Indian Territory on January 9, 1897 and it was directed that all the original papers be immediately forwarded to the court to be used and considered in the case of Callie Newberry et al v Chickasaw Nation

He further finds that the case was docketed on the citizenship docket of the United States court for the southern district of the Indian Territory as citizenship case No 85, and entitled Callie Newberry v Chickasaw Nation

He finds from the records of his office that the original papers filed with the Commission on September 9 1896, were transmitted to the clerk of the United States court in conformity with the notice of appeal of January 9 1897 and the receipt of the clerk of the court therefor was forwarded to the Commission on February 5 1897 He transmits for the information of the Department the notice of appeal and receipt of the clerk of the United States court for all of the papers found in the files of his office in reference to the 1896 citizenship case of Callie Newberry

He further reports that there is no entry on the records of his office of any additional consideration or disposition of the case by the United States court until an order of dismissal by the court entered on January 15 1900 a certified copy of which he transmits for the information of the Department

Mr Bixby says that after the receipt of Departmental letter of July 11 1906, he requested the clerk of the United States court for the southern district of the Indian Territory to furnish a certified copy of all the docket entries in the case of Callie Newberry v Chickasaw Nation United States court southern district citizenship case No 85 and the clerk furnished him a certified copy of the docket entries on September 7 1906 which is inclosed

Mr Bixby explains that the original records in the majority of the citizenship cases appealed from the decisions of the Commission in 1896 to the United States court were destroyed in a fire which consumed the United States court-house at Ardmore in the year 1897 He expresses the belief that the original papers filed with the Commission on September 9 1896 were thus destroyed but he says that the clerk of the court has furnished him with what purported to be copies of the original papers filed in this case and which are all the records in his office in reference thereto These papers are transmitted for the use of the Department

He also says it is to be noted that in the copy of the affidavit of Callie Newberry, which purports to have been sworn to on August 31 1896 the following allegation is made

'I have seven children living, their names are Sam Willie Louis, Calvin Mariah, Lula and Lydia Newberry

and he requests that this matter receive the consideration of the Department and that the papers be returned to his office as they were temporarily withdrawn from the records of the office of the clerk of the United States court for consideration in replying to Departmental letter of July 11 1906 He particularly notes that there is nothing in the records of the Commission or of his office which would in any manner indicate that any other person was named in the original petition in 1896 citizenship case No 111, and filed with the Commission on September 9 of that year than the petitioner Callie Newberry

The records of the Commission and of his office failing to show that any application had been made for the enrollment of the persons named by Mr Lee in his petition of February 12 1906, as citizens by blood of the Chickasaw Nation prior to December 25 1902 the Commissioner says that Mr Lee now seeks to invoke the aid of the records of the United States court for the purpose of showing that such an application was made under the provisions of the act of June 10 1896

The Commissioner quotes from section 4 of the act of Congress approved April 26, 1906, supra, as follows

"That no name shall be transferred from the approved freedmen or any other approved rolls of the Choctaw, Chickasaw Creek, or Seminole tribes, respectively, to the roll of citizens by blood, unless the records in charge of the Commissioner to the Five Civilized Tribes show that application for enrollment as a citizen by blood was made within the time prescribed by law by or for the party seeking

the transfer, and said records shall be conclusive evidence as to the fact of such application, unless it be shown by documentary evidence that the Commission to the Five Civilized Tribes actually received such application within the time prescribed by law. "
and says that this provision of the act, in his opinion, prohibits the transfer of the names of persons from the approved rolls of Choctaw and Chickasaw freedmen to the rolls of citizens by blood of the Choctaw and Chickasaw nations, unless application for enrollment as citizens by blood of either of the nations was made on or before December 24, 1902, the time prescribed by law for the termination of the reception of applications for enrollment in these two nations.

He says he does not consider that the copy of the affidavit of Callie Newberry of August 31, 1896, can in any manner be construed as an application made under the act of June 10, 1896, for citizenship in the Chickasaw Nation of her seven children— Sam, Willie, Louis, Calvin, Mariah, Lula, and Lydia Newberry; but, admitting for the sake of argument that this affidavit of Callie Newberry is construed as an application submitted on behalf of these persons for citizenship in the Chickasaw Nation under the act approved June 10, 1896, he is of the opinion that they would be bound by the decision of the Commission of November 10, 1896, denying the petition filed by Callie Newberry on September 9, 1896.

He gives it as his opinion that the Commission did have jurisdiction over these persons under the act of 1896, if they applied for admission to citizenship in the Chickasaw Nation, and the decision of November 10, 1896, would have been determinate as to their right to citizenship in the nation.

He cites the fact that the Department held, on May 25, 1906 I. T. D., 9114-1906), in the Cherokee enrollment case of Laura E. Akin et al., that—

"As the Commission to the Five Civilized Tribes had jurisdiction when it denied, under the provisions of the act of Congress of June 10, 1896 (29 Stat. L., 21), the principal applicant's application for recognition as a citizen of the Cherokee Nation, there could be no 'continuing application,' as contended by the attorney for the claimants."

It is the opinion of the Commissioner that Mr. Lee is seeking to establish that an application was made within the time prescribed by law for the persons named in the petition of February 12, 1906, as defined by section 4 of the act of April 26, 1906, and that Mr. Lee has failed to show that these people come within the provisions of the law, and recommends that his decision of June 14, 1906, denying the petition, be affirmed.

In this connection he also acknowledges the receipt of departmental letter of September 6, 1906 (I. T. D. 7227, 12724-1906) in reference to the petition for the transfer of the name of Delbert Green from the roll of Choctaw freedmen to the roll of citizens by blood of the Choctaw Nation, and in which action was suspended by the Department until a report was submitted by the Commissioner showing whether application was made for Delbert Green for citizenship in the Choctaw Nation under the act of Congress approved June 10, 1896, and directing that specific information of like character be furnished in all similar cases where the date of the application is material.

He reports in that connection that in the consideration of petitions for the transfer of the names of persons from the approved rolls of Choctaw and Chickasaw freedmen to the rolls of citizens by blood of the two nations, examination has been made of the records of petitions for citizenship in the Choctaw and Chickasaw cases submitted under the act of Congress approved June 10, 1896, and that the findings of fact in those decisions that application was not made within the time prescribed by law is a correct reflection of the records of his office, but it is possible however, that in a few cases similar to the one under discussion and where the original papers filed in 1896 have been transferred to the United States court, such petitions may have included the names of persons who do not appear on the 1896 citizenship records of the Commission.

He expresses himself as being firmly of the opinion that the Commission, under the act of June 10, 1896, acquired jurisdiction over all persons who applied for admission to citizenship in the Choctaw and Chickasaw nations under the provisions of that act, who had not theretofore been recognized citizens of either of the tribes, by having their names placed on some tribal roll of such citizens, or being duly and lawfully admitted to citizenship by some constituted authority of either of the nations, and that the decisions adverse to such persons were final.

Mr. Bixby holds that the petitions submitted on behalf of Choctaw and Chickasaw freedmen for admission to citizenship in the Choctaw and Chickasaw nations under the act of Congress approved June 10, 1896, and which were denied, can not, as held by the Department in its letter of May 25, 1906 (I. T. D. 9114-1906), be construed as "continuing applications" as contemplated by section 4, of the act of Congress approved April 26, 1906.

In connection with the petition filed by Mr. Lee on February 12, 1906, for the transfer of the names of Calvin Newberry et al. from the roll of Chickasaw freedmen to the roll of citizens by blood of the Chickasaw Nation, Mr. Bixby says he desires to invite attention to departmental letter of December 4, 1905, (I. T. D. 16096–1905), denying the petitions submitted by Charles von Weise, of Ardmore, for the transfer of the names of Lula Stevenson et al., Louis Newberry et al., Willie Newberry et al., Nelson Colbert, Stephen Alexander et al., and Sampson Alexander et al. from the roll of Chickasaw freedmen to the roll of citizens by blood of the Chickasaw Nation. He also transmits a supplemental motion in the case of Lula Stevenson et al. Willie Newberry et al., and Louis Newberry et al., filed in his office by Mr. von Weise on December 12, 1905.

He also transmits for the consideration of the Department in connection with the petition, the petition transmitted June 14, 1906, in the case of Calvin Newberry and supplemental petition filed in his office on March 5, 1906, by Albert J. Lee, on behalf of Willie Newberry, as administrator of the estate of Lydia Newberry, deceased, for the transfer of the name of Lydia Newberry from the roll of Chickasaw freedmen to the roll of citizens by blood of the Chickasaw Nation.

Finally, he says the statements contained in his order or decision of June 14, 1906, are applicable to this latter petition, and he invites attention to the fact that the person on whose behalf the petition is submitted appears in the copy of the affidavit of Callie Newberry of August 31, 1896, as Lydia Newberry.

The Commissioner submits proof of the fact that Calvin Newberry did in 1896 make application for the enrollment as citizens of the Chickasaw Nation of his children, Sam, Willie, Louis, Calvin, Mariah, Lula, and Lydia Newberry, basing his claim for right to enrollment on his descent from Ben Love, his father, who was a half-breed Chickasaw Indian. His claim was contested by the Chickasaw Nation on the ground that he was a freedman who had been held in slavery and was not entitled to recognition or enrollment as a citizen by blood of the nation. On the issues thus joined his case was tried, and the Commission to the Five Civilized Tribes determined that the applicants were not entitled to enrollment as citizens by blood of that nation. The case having been appealed to the United States court from the adverse decision of the Commission, the applicants failed to prosecute their appeal, and it was dismissed for want of prosecution. In that manner, under the law then in force, the decision of the Commission became final.

The Commissioner gives no history of the subsequent application under which these persons were enrolled as Chickasaw freedmen, nor does he submit a copy of the proof on which the enrollment was predicated. From his explanation of the manner of procedure in his office in cases of this character, it must be assumed that the proof subsequently submitted in no way tended to sustain a claim that these persons were Chickasaws by blood, but did satisfactorily establish their right to enrollment as Chickasaw freedmen. While it would have been much more satisfactory to have had a copy of the proof submitted on that question, the office assumes that adequate examination has been made and that a preponderance of the evidence which was submitted to the Commission or commissioner was to the effect that these persons were not of Chickasaw blood, but were, in fact, Chickasaw freedmen.

For these reasons the office recommends that the application for the transfer of the persons named in the application of Calvin Newberry be denied.

Under the report of the Commissioner it is assumed that there is no proof in his office, nor has there ever been, showing that the other parties applicant who are mentioned in this case have applied for or established their right to enrollment as Chickasaws by blood within the time provided by law. It is therefore recommended that the Commissioner's decision as to these persons be approved and that the application be denied.

Very respectfully,   C. F. LARRABEE, Acting Commissioner.

DEPARTMENT OF THE INTERIOR,
Washington, December 13, 1906.
COMMISSIONER TO THE FIVE CIVILIZED TRIBES,
Muscogee, Ind. T.

SIR: December 3, 1906, the Indian Office submitted your report of September 19, 1906, relative to the petition of Calvin Newberry et al.

On June 14, 1906, you denied the petition for the transfer of the names of said Calvin Newberry and his minor children, Ethel and Mabelle Newberry; Simon Newberry and his minor children, Isom, Bertha, Ben, Lillie, and Mary Newberry; Willie Newberry and his minor children, Effie, Wiley, Willie, and Sadie Newberry; Louis Newberry and his minor child, Lula Newberry; Mira Stevenson and her minor child, Grady Stevenson; Lula Stevenson and her minor child, Loan Stevenson, from the roll of Chickasaw freedmen to the roll of citizens by blood of the Chickasaw Nation, as it did not appear from the records of your office that any application was made for the enrollment of the petitioners, or any of them, as citizens by blood of the Chickasaw Nation prior to December 25, 1902.

June 20, 1906, the attorney for the petitioners transmitted to the Department his affidavit wherein he alleges that the docket of citizenship cases in the office of the clerk of the United States court for the southern district of the Indian Territory shows that application was made on August 31, 1896, by Callie Newberry for the enrollment of herself and Sam, Willie, Louis, Calvin, Mariah, Lula, and Lydia Newberry for citizenship in the Chickasaw Nation to the Commission to the Five Civilized Tribes under the act of June 10, 1896 (29 Stats., 321).

You find from an examination of the records of the Commission to the Five Civilized Tribes, in reference to applications submitted under the provisions of the act of June 10, 1896, that there was filed with the Commission on September 9, 1896, a petition of Callie Newberry, praying for admission to citizenship in the Chickasaw Nation, and that on November 10, 1896, an order was entered by the Commission denying the petition; that this case appears on the 1896 citizenship docket of the Commission as No. 111, Callie Newberry v. the Chickasaw Nation. You informed the Department that the original petition in the case is not in the possession of your office and is not believed to be now in existence; but you find that from the decision rendered by the Commission November 10, 1896, an appeal was taken to the United States court for the southern district of the Indian Territory, and that the case was docketed on the citizenship docket of the court as citizenship case No. 85, entitled Callie Newberry v. the Chickasaw Nation. It also appears from the records of your office that the original papers, filed with the Commission on September 9, 1896, were transmitted to the clerk of the court in conformity with a notice of appeal of January 9, 1897. You report that there is no entry on the records of your office of any additional consideration or disposition of the case by the court until an order of dismissal by the court, entered on January 15, 1900. It appears that the original records in the majority of the citizenship cases appealed from the decision of the Commission in 1896 to this United States court were destroyed in a fire which consumed the United States court-house at Ardmore in 1897. You expressed the belief that the original papers filed with the Commission on September 9, 1896, were thus destroyed. The clerk of the court, however, has furnished you with what purport to be copies of the original papers filed in this case. The copy of an alleged affidavit of Callie Newberry, which purports to have been sworn to August 31, 1896, is, in part, as follows:

"I was born and raised in the Indian Territory. My father and mother's name is Ben and Mariah Love. My father, Ben Love, is a half-breed Chickasaw Indian. I have seven children living, their names are Sam, Willie, Louis, Calvin, Mariah, Lula, and Lydia Newberry."

There is, you find, nothing in the records of the Commission to the Five Civilized Tribes or of your office which would in any manner indicate that any other persons were named in the original petition in 1896 and filed with the Commission to the Five Civilized Tribes on September 9 of that year than Callie Newberry. This would seem to be correct.

Referring to section 4 of the act of April 26, 1906 (34 Stat. L., 137), you conclude that the copy of the affidavit of Callie Newberry of August 31, 1896, can not in any manner be considered as an application made under the act of June 10, 1896, for citizenship in the Chickasaw Nation of her seven children, Sam, Willie, Louis, Calvin, Mariah, Lula, and Lydia Newberry, but that, admitting that the alleged affidavit of Callie Newberry can be construed as an application submitted on behalf of these persons for citizenship in said nation under the act of June 10, 1896, you are of the opinion that they would be bound by the decision of the Commission of November 10, 1896.

You assert that the Commission had jurisdiction over these persons under the act of 1896 if they applied for admission to citizenship in said nation, and the decision of November 10, 1896, would have been determinative as to their right to citizenship in the nation.

This does not altogether agree with the views expressed in the approved opinion of the Assistant Attorney-General of September 26, 1906, in the case of Hayn Nelms, in which it was stated that—

"the adjudication or admission of Nelms to citizenship by intermarriage, made by the Commission in 1896, was, under the act of June 28, 1898, reviewable and subject to correction by the Commission. The Commission is a continuing administrative tribunal, having quasi-judicial powers, and the general rule is that such tribunals may review and correct their former judgments. * * * The act of June 28, 1898, expressly granted to the Commission power to scrutinize and to purge the tribal rolls and to enroll only such as may have lawful right thereto. That included their own roll and their own action, as well as the rolls and action of the tribal authorities."

The Indian Office, in its letter of December 3, 1906, for reasons stated, concurs in your recommendation that the petition under consideration be denied.

Section 4 of the act of April 26, 1906, is as follows:

"That no name shall be transferred from the approved freedmen or any other approved rolls of the Choctaw, Chickasaw, Cherokee, Creek, or Seminole tribes, respectively, to the roll of citizens by blood, unless the records in charge of the Commissioner to the Five Civilized Tribes show that application for enrollment as a citizen by blood was made within the time prescribed by law by or for the party seeking the transfer; and said records shall be conclusive evidence as to the fact of such application, unless it be shown by documentary evidence that the Commission to the Five Civilized Tribes actually received such application within the time prescribed by law."

It is not clear upon what grounds the principal applicant, Callie Newberry, in 1896, based her claims (even admitting that such affidavit as that alleged to have been made August 31, 1896, was filed with the Commission to the Five Civilized Tribes), whether by virtue of her Indian blood or as a Chickasaw freedman. She was 50 years of age at that time. It seems that none of the persons named in said alleged affidavit has been enrolled or duly recognized as a citizen of the Chickasaw Nation by blood or as a freedman, except on the freedman roll made by the Commission to the Five Civilized Tribes. If the application of 1896 was for enrollment as a Chickasaw freedman, it can not, of course, be considered as an application for enrollment of the parties as citizens by blood. Furthermore, it is considered that, even if the application of 1896 could be accepted as an application for enrollment of the parties mentioned in the alleged affidavit of August 31, 1896, as citizens by blood, they elected to be enrolled on the freedman roll by the Commission to the Five Civilized Tribes, and have forfeited any right, if any they may have had, as citizens by blood.

Apparently, however, under no circumstances can they be enrolled as citizens by blood, as none of them have been duly recognized as such citizens by legally constituted authority, or enrolled as such citizen on the rolls of the Chickasaw Nation.

The petitions in the matter of Calvin Newberry et al., are denied, and also the other petitions and motions received with your letter. You will make a separate report relative to the application of Delbert Green for transfer of his name from the roll of Choctaw freedmen to the roll of citizens by blood of the Choctaw Nation, mentioned in your letter of September 17, 1906.

A copy of Indian Office letter of December 3, 1906 (Land 83245), is inclosed. You will observe that an error is made therein on page 11 as to the principal applicant to the application of 1896.

The petitions you wished returned to be returned to the court are inclosed. The other papers have been sent to the Indian Office.

Respectfully,
JESSE E. WILSON,
Assistant Secretary.

Through the Commissioner of Indian Affairs.

The New York Indians *v.* the United States. No. 17861. Court of Claims. Decided May 15, 1905.

OPINION OF THE COURT.

Nott, chief justice, delivered the opinion of the court:

1. The cause of action confided to the jurisdiction of this court is thus defined by the act of 28th of January, 1893 (27 Stat. L., p. 426): The claim "of those Indians who were parties to the treaty of Buffalo Creek, growing out of the alleged unexecuted stipulations of the treaty on the part of the United States."

2. The unexecuted stipulations of the treaty on the part of the United States were these: By the treaty the United States agreed to set apart 1,824,000 acres of land "as a permanent home for all the New York Indians." Such of the tribes as did not "accept and agree to remove to the country set apart for their homes within five years" were to "forfeit all interest in the lands set apart." None of the tribes moved or was removed to the country set apart, none of them made a demand or request for removal, some of them positively refused to remove when requested by agents and commissioners of the United States, others of them denied that they were parties to the treaty and averred that it had been procured in their names by corruption and fraud. After twenty-two years thus passed, the United States declared the lands open for public entry and sold them. But the treaty chanced to be in such form that the

Supreme Court construed it to be a grant in presenti, and held that the United States, not having declared a forfeiture, the title remained in the Indians who were parties to the treaty, and that they were entitled to recover the avails of the land, amounting to $1,967,056. (170 U. S. R., 1. 173 id., 161.)

The action, therefore, is substantially one to recover money had and received by the defendants to the use of the plaintiffs, and the primary question now before the court is: To whom shall this money be paid? Who were the parties, within the intent of the treaty, that are entitled to receive it?

3. If the Indians had removed to the West, as contemplated by the treaty, the different tribes would have received tracts of land proportionate to their numbers, and the members of the tribes would have held as communal owners. The present suit is not to recover land, but money, the proceeds of land, the title of which land was vested in the Indians as communal owners. The proceeds therefore, in the matter of disposition must follow the rule which would have governed the disposition of the land. The Government, as guardian of the Indians, might have treated the proceeds as a fund to be retained by the guardian, the income to be paid to the communal owners per capita, or it might have treated the funds as Indian lands have been treated, by partitioning them by personal allotment among the communal owners. It has substantially selected the last course. The intent is that each communal owner of the land who would have been entitled under the treaty to 320 acres if the lands were allotted shall recover his proportionate part of the fund.

4. In determining who are communal owners entitled to be paid per capita the court will follow Indian laws and customs so far as they do not come in conflict with the laws of the United States or the purposes of the treaty or with natural law and justice.

The court will therefore adhere so far as possible to the fundamental Indian law of communal ownership, and will respect, as long as it does not conflict with the purposes of the treaty, the tribal determination of membership, but the court must at the same time recognize the fact that an Indian community is not the intact thing which it once was, and that communal ownership is not the well-defined ascertainable estate or interest which it was when there were real communities living in unity and communal possession on communal lands. The changes which had taken place in 1860 when these lands were open to purchase, had even then nearly obliterated the old communal lines, and the changes which have since come have reduced some, if not all, of those communities to little more than voluntary societies held together by the annuities paid by the Government per capita. Thus for instance, the Oneidas were once a powerful tribe of the Six Nations. They have been divided and subdivided into the New York Oneidas, the Canadian Oneidas, and the Wisconsin Oneidas; and the New York Oneidas have been subdivided into two "Christian parties" and two "Orchard parties." There are also Oneidas living upon the Onondaga Reservation and Oneidas living upon their own lands, and Oneidas to whom lands have been allotted in severalty and who have become citizens of the State of New York and who have ceased to be, in a political sense, Indians. To accept as final the determination of such communities or societies on the question of a legal right to participate in the funds would be an evasion of judicial duty. It would be committing individual rights to the incompetent hands of those who have a direct pecuniary interest in the decision. Neither can the court accept the action of any community subsequent to the date of the treaty as being a legal determination on the question of communal membership; and where it appears that since the execution of the treaty a communal roll has been tampered with and persons who were not Indians have been admitted to communal membership from improper motives and by arbitrary methods, the court will not regard them as beneficiaries under the treaty or as persons entitled to participate in the fund within the intent of the jurisdictional statute.

5. The treaty of Buffalo Creek, as has been said, was a grant in praesenti of the lands west of the Mississippi, but it was also an executory contract between the parties. The intent was (which was the chief consideration for the contract) that all the New York Indians should remove west and should receive all the lands designated, and that they should do so within five years; and that if they should fail to do so the contract should come to an end by the United States declaring a forfeiture, in which case it was expressly provided that the Indians should "forfeit all interest in the lands so set apart." The lands so set apart were 1,824,000 acres, and the acreage was ascertained by taking the number of all persons belonging to the tribe, so far as known, amounting to 5,485, and adding thereto 215 (apparently for nonenumerated Indians), and allowing to each person 320 acres of land.

6. The persons therefore, to be removed to the West and to receive 320 acres of land each, or a communal interest therein, were the Indian communities (embracing by that term all persons affiliated with the Indians) whom the United States desired to

remove west of the Mississippi. The United States were not interested in academic questions of Indian blood or Indian citizenship. Whether an Indian family of half bloods residing on an Indian reservation in the State of New York or the State of Wisconsin were children of white men or of white women was, for the purposes of the contract, abstract, and irrelevant. That one such family should be called Indian and be allowed to go to the West to acquire lands of the United States, but that the other should be called white and not be allowed to go or to acquire lands, would be an incongruity utterly foreign to the intent of the agreement.

It is true that the Iroquois, as with almost all Indian tribes, descent was through the mother. The Iroquois woman was the daughter of the tribe unchangeably, irrevocably. She could not marry within the tribe, for all who were born of the daughters of a tribe were brothers and sisters. When she married it was her husband who came to dwell in her tribe, and not she who passed over to his. If she married a white man she might live in his house and home, but when he died she could return to her kindred. Maid, wife, or widow, the Iroquois woman was always a daughter of her tribe, and her children were sons and daughters of her tribe; and they, with the sons and daughters of her tribal sisters, alone could be members of her tribe by birthright. Therefore it was that the daughters of the tribe were the mothers of the tribe, and they only. No man could be a son of the tribe unless he was a son of a daughter of the tribe. The Indians, therefore, held that as a white woman was not the daughter of a tribe, she, on the death of her husband, had no tribe; that she was what she had been—a stranger, an alien, an outcast, and not an Indian. It followed that her children were what she was, exiles without a tribe, and strangers, not of Indian blood.

This was the logical, the inexorable result of Indian law; but the practical results which would come from attempting to carry out the purpose of the treaty according to this Indian law instead of according to the manifest purpose of the contracting parties is well illustrated in a case stated by claimant's counsel. A full-blooded Seneca Indian married a white woman. The daughter of that union was in fact one-half Indian, but according to Seneca law wholly white. She married a full-blooded Seneca, and her daughter, three-fourths Indian, was still, by Seneca law, wholly white. Her daughter, three-fourths Indian, married a full-blooded Seneca, and her daughter, seven-eighths Indian, was still, according to Seneca law, wholly white. Finally the children of this woman, though their father might be a full-blooded Seneca Indian, and they have fifteen-sixteenths Seneca blood in their veins, would still, in Indian legal estimation, be wholly white.

7. In what manner the numbers of the different tribes set forth in Schedule A, annexed to the treaty, were ascertained is now unknown; but it was for the interest of the United States that all persons affiliated with an Indian community should go, and it was for the interest of the Indians that there should be land enough for all. Whether the census in Schedule A included white wives and their children is not certain, but in view of the intent and purpose of the treaty it must be presumed that it did, and it is certain, apart from such presumption, that there was a considerable margin of land, 68,800 acres, reserved for the Indians over and above the sum total of population enumerated in Schedule A. Such being the manifest purpose of the treaty, and such the means for carrying it into effect, some claimants can not now be allowed to come in and say that the sum total of the acreage now represented by the proceeds of land ($1,967,056) was intended for only such persons as were technically citizens or communal owners in the Six Nations. In determining who were the persons termed Indians within the intent of the treaty, the court must resort to the actual communities then existing, so far as they can be ascertained, and must carry out the obvious intent of the treaty without being limited by Indian laws or customs which would defeat its chief purpose.

8. The two important dates in this case are 1838, when the treaty was entered into, and 1860, when the United States opened the lands to public entry and deprived the Indians of their title without having declared a forfeiture. If, shortly after the signing of the treaty, all of the Indians had been removed to the West and all of the tract had been turned over to them, no one can doubt but that the United States would have required and the Indians would have consented to the removal of every member of each Indian community without regard to blood or citizenship or the Indian law of descent; and if shortly before 1860 the Indians had then determined to go West, it can not be doubted but that the United States would have expected and required that all of the Indian communities as then existed should remove if all of the land was to be enjoyed by them.

During that twenty-two years there was disintegration and change in each community, and during that twenty-two years the agreement was kept alive by the inaction of the parties, by the failure of one of them to declare a forfeiture. The question, "Who are the community?" continued during that twenty-two years, and it would have been answered at the end as at the beginning. If, in 1859 both parties had determined to carry the treaty into effect, there would have remained the same intent which existed when the treaty was made—that all persons attached to an Indian community should go and should be provided for. The United States wished the one; the Indians expected the other. Consequently, the court must adopt a rule of descent or participation which would embrace all persons whom it was the policy of the United States to remove; and this rule being ex necessitate rei, once established must continue A court can not have one rule for one period of time and another for another period of time. The white wife and her children born between 1838 and 1860 were as much Indians within the intent of the treaty as any full-blooded Indian in the Six Nations; and what was the rule during that period of time must continue to be the rule up to the time of the judgment or the satisfaction of it; that is to say, the children of white mothers and Indian fathers affiliated with the tribes must be reckoned as Indians. The court must look upon the community and its members as such, and can not turn aside into the genealogy of individuals or be turned aside by the peculiarities of Indian laws and customs. This is not a question of Indian citizenship or tribal custom or communal ownership in Indian property, but simply a question of contract of the subject-matter and purpose of a contract, and of the intent of those who entered into it.

9. The treaty of Buffalo Creek was between nine tribes, bands, or subdivisions of Indians, signatories to the treaty as such. The present consideration moving to the United States from the Indians was the cession by these "several tribes of New York Indians" to the United States of all their right, title, and interest to certain lands secured to them at Green Bay, Wis., by the treaty of 1831. "In consideration of the above cession and relinquishment, and in order to manifest the deep interest of the United States in the future peace and prosperity of the New York Indians," the United States agreed to set apart a tract of country west of the State of Missouri " as a permanent home for all the New York Indians now residing in the State of New York, or in Wisconsin, or elsewhere in the United States, who have no permanent homes." Annexed to the treaty is a "census of the New York Indians as taken in 1837," made before the execution of the treaty (Schedule A). This refers more particularly to residence and contains eleven subdivisions of New York Indians, but all of them residing in New York and Wisconsin.

Who, then, are the beneficiaries under the second article of the treaty? Primarily, of course, the New York Indians who executed the treaty "now residing in the State of New York or in Wisconsin;" but the treaty adds an ambiguous term, "or elsewhere in the United States," with an ambiguous limitation. "who have no permanent homes."

The primary purpose of the treaty being to remove all Indians from the East to the West, and the secondary purpose to gather up New York Indians who might not be residing in New York or Wisconsin but who had no fixed domicile or no affiliation with other tribes (in the words of the treaty, who had "no permanent homes"), it must be held that such persons, and only such persons, are the beneficiaries and entitled to participate in the fund. That is to say, Indians who had acquired a permanent home with other tribes or who had become more or less affiliated with them, or who were not represented by signatories to the treaty, or who did not relinquish lands in Wisconsin, or who did not signify an intent to return to a New York tribe or to actually remove to the ceded lands before 1860, can not be regarded as "Indians who were parties to the treaty of Buffalo Creek" within the intent of the jurisdictional act. By the term "permanent homes" we understand something in the nature of domicile, and by a change of domicile we understand that such Indians lost their old domicile and severed their connection with their former tribe and ceased to be communal owners in tribal property. A more specific designation can be given, but this states the principles upon which the ruling will rest.

10. The Oneidas, of Ontario, Canada, were domiciles and living in New York in 1838, and were then parties to and beneficiaries under the treaty. In 1842 they sold their lands in New York and moved across the border into Canada. The number who went (320) and the number who remained (300) were about equal. Their going was before the breach of the agreement and while the Government was anxious and willing to remove all New York Indians to the West. Did they, by moving across the border, forfeit all rights to be removed? Or were they free to move back across the border prior to 1860 and be among those who might be removed west of the Mississippi? And what rights have they within the intent and meaning of the decision of the Supreme Court?

The judgment ($1,967,056) which the Supreme Court has directed in favor of the claimants represents 1,824,000 acres of land, reserved by the treaty of 1838, and those 1,824,000 acres of land represent the 5,485 Indians enumerated in Schedule A of the treaty and 215 Indians not enumerated in the schedule. The Supreme Court has decided that the claimants are entitled to recover this gross amount of $1,967,056, but has not directed this court to so distribute it that one man shall recover another man's money or that one portion of a tribe shall recover the damages suffered by another portion. It did lie in the mouth of the defendants, the United States, to say that the Oneidas in Canada had forfeited their right to recover, but it does not lie in the mouth of the other Oneidas to say that they are entitled to both their own and the others' damages.

If the 300 Oneidas who remained in New York had been removed west of the Mississippi immediately after the 320 passed over the border into Canada, it is inconceivable that they would have been awarded land for 620 Oneidas. If the Oneidas of New York have no right to recover for the lands of the 320, has the Government done anything to declare a forfeiture on the part of the 320?

Our Indians are and have been the wards of the United States, and the Indian has no right of expatriation. Whether they may or may not leave the country is a question of Indian policy. In Sitting Bull's case they removed to Canada with the intent of remaining there, and became domiciled so far as Indians could be. The Indian policy required that they should be brought back, and they were brought back. In the case of the Kickapoos, they removed to Mexico with like intent to remain and be domiciled there. The Indian policy required that they be brought back, and they were brought back. In 1842 the Indian policy might have required that the Oneidas be brought back, and if it had, they would have been brought back. They did not cease to be wards of the United States because they had crossed the border and attempted to domicile themselves in a foreign country; and it was expressly held in the case of Lowe r. Kickapoos (37 C. Cls. R., 413) that "the Indians being wards of the United States can not suspend that relation without the consent of the Government." There was no law which prohibited these Oneidas from returning; they had sold their land, but the Senecas might have thrown open their doors as did the Cayugas; the United States took no act to sanction their expatriation or to deprive them of their rights under the treaty, and those rights continued until the breach of the agreement in 1860. From an equitable point of view it may be added that they did more to carry out the policy of the United States by removing from the State of New York than any of the Indians who are now represented in this court.

The facts to be noted in relation to these Oneidas of Ontario are these: There was no individual emigration; it was not the case of an individual here and there withdrawing himself from the community and ceasing to be a member of it, leaving the community intact. On the contrary, by communal consent a part of the tribe separated from the other part, taking with them their portion of the communal property. Politically they were not expatriated; they did not become citizens of Canada. Some of them returned to the State of New York, and some of them returned to the United States, going to Wisconsin.

It is settled by the decree of the Supreme Court that these Indians had acquired in 1838 an undivided legal estate in the western lands. It seems tolerably clear that the separation of these Indians as a distinct part of the Oneida community by mutual consent, retaining their share of other communal property, did not work a transfer of their interest in the lands west of the Mississippi to that part of the community which remained behind. After the decision of the Supreme Court it can not be said that the United States declared a forfeiture against them, either because they removed to Canada or because they failed to remove west of the Mississippi. How, then, could their title have been divested, with no act of forfeiture on the part of the United States? It may be said that their removal from the guardianship of the United States created a personal disability to maintain an action against the United States. This may be true, and might perhaps be upheld if the United States had said so. The effect of the statute is to allow all of the Indians to recover for all of the land sold, and the court can neither say that a portion of the Indians may recover for all of the land sold, nor say that the land of some of these Indians has, in some indescribable way, become forfeited to the United States, nor that some Indians who were parties to the treaty of Buffalo Creek are not to be admitted within the jurisdiction of the court.

11. The rolls prepared under the direction of the Secretary of the Interior in this case would be absolutely right and accurate if the questions in the case were those of Indian citizenship or communal ownership, or related exclusively to Indian property and rights.

The court appreciates the work done by direction of the Secretary of the Interior, and regrets that there should be a difference of opinion as to the distribution of the fund; but for the reasons hereinbefore given the court can not regard this as simply a distribution of Indian property by Indian methods according to Indian law and at the dictation of Indian communities. The court, acting judicially, must be controlled by the purpose of the treaty and the terms of the jurisdictional act. It can not exclude from rolls Indians who were or whose ancestors were parties to the treaty of Buffalo Creek and it can not admit as beneficiaries Indians who were not parties to the treaty of Buffalo Creek and whose ancestors were not. Neither can the court uphold the unsatisfactory if not fictitious rolls which some of the parties have framed, nor can the court allow Indian law or custom or decision to determine who shall participate in the distribution of this fund and in effect decide who were persons intended to be removed from New York and Wisconsin to the country west of the Mississippi.

For the reasons subsequently stated the court is also of the opinion that the rolls by separate tribes or bodies of communal owners, giving different amounts to the members of different communities will have to be so recast as to bring all participants to one common amount.

But the court is of the opinion that the limit set by the Secretary of the Interior within which parties were required to appear and present their claims is sound in principle and that the limit named by him, the 31st of December 1901, must be upheld. When a fund is to be distributed equally among many persons it is inevitable that there must be a day of distribution, and where the fund to be distributed is communal property it is likewise inevitable that the day of distribution must be one arbitrarily fixed which will enable the officers of a court or other custodians of the fund to ascertain the number of recipients and the amount of expenses which will be a charge upon the fund and to ascertain the names and individual rights of the recipients. The court regards the action of the Secretary in the steps taken by him to notify parties to come in and in the selection of the day named as not only reasonable, but as eminently just and wise.

12. The most doubtful and most perplexing question in this case (which is crowded with perplexing questions) is, "Upon what basis shall the distribution of the fund be made?" Three have been suggested.

The first is to regard the communal property as having vested personally in the communal owners at the time when the treaty was executed (or perhaps more properly, at the time when the United States sold the lands) and then to trace down, individually and personally, per stirpes, the descendants of those original owners, and decree payment to them per capita in the different amounts which family changes and vicissitudes must have brought about.

There are two objections to this. When it is remembered that communal ownership extends equally to men and women and children and infants in arms it is apparent that to determine with precision who were the communal owners in different groups and scattered homes of more than 5,000 Indians on a given day forty-five or sixty-seven years ago would be an absolute impossibility. The other objection is that this fund, being Indian property, the court should so far as possible, conform to Indian law, and especially to that great fundamental principle of Indian law—communal and not individual ownership.

The second basis is to take the census denominated "Schedule A," annexed to the treaty as a guide and to regard the Indians (5,485 in number) as forming 11 distinct communities and to apportion the fund among them in proportion to the number shown by the census thereby making 11 communal funds to be divided each among the individuals now forming actually or constructively these 11 communities.

The third basis is to regard all of the Indians who were parties to the treaty as one community and to distribute the fund among all the Indians and descendants of Indians now existing, share and share alike.

As to the second basis it may be conceded that the treaty (article 2) contemplated two things, viz, that the Indians would actually remove to their future home beyond the Mississippi and that the lands there should be "divided equally among them according to their respective numbers as mentioned in the schedule hereunto annexed" (the census, Schedule A). Previously, in the same article, the treaty had mentioned 1,824,000 acres of land as the tract granted "being 320 acres for each soul of said Indians, as their numbers are at present computed." The numbers mentioned in Schedule A multiplied by 320 give an acreage of but 1,755,200 acres, leaving an excess of 68,800 acres. This excess was probably intended for Indians who might have been overlooked in the enumeration of the census. It is at the same time manifest that all of these eleven communities could not be moved westward in one day and told to divide their lands among themselves in proportion to their respective numbers, but that they would be moved in small bodies, and on their arrival have allotted to them quantities of lands at the rate of 320 acres to each emigrant. Other provisions of the treaty also show that it was contemplated that some of the tribes might not remove, and as to them the third article provided that those who did not remove "within five years, or such other time as the President may from time to time appoint, shall forfeit all interest in the land so set apart." In a word the grant was en bloc, but the treaty contemplated the removal of nine or eleven distinct communities, with distinct allotments of land in proportion to their numbers.

The Secretary of the Interior has proceeded upon this theory in preparing rolls in this case, and if the fund is to be distributed only among those Indians who were annuitants and on the rolls of the Indian Office, this theory would have very strong support in those facts. The objections to it are, first, that it ends in an inequitable result. According to it one community of Indians—the Oneidas—will receive more than $1,000 per capita, and another—the Stockbridges and Munsees—only $147 per capita. It would be irrational to attribute this immense difference of 747 per cent to natural causes. It is manifest that there has been an error in the past computation, or that there has been emigration from tribe to tribe, or that something other than natural growth has brought about this immense disparity in the result.

Another objection to the second basis relates back to the true intent of the treaty that true intent unquestionably was that every Indian emigrant or beneficiary under the treaty should receive at least 320 acres of land without reference to the number of persons in his tribe or the number of members in his family. That the true intent was not carried out was due to the inaction of both parties. The treaty contemplated keeping the tribes on separate allotments of land, but the primary and paramount intent was, as stated, that each Indian beneficiary should receive at least 320 acres of land. The provisions for segregating the tribes and giving each his own share founded upon 320 acres for each individual were not antagonistic or alternative to the primary intent, but in furtherance of it. If the treaty had been carried into effect within five years as contemplated there would have been no dispute whatever upon this point. Such being the intent of the treaty, the question is whether inaction of the parties and the sale of lands and the substitution of the fund for the land are to change this primary basis of distribution.

The communal changes referred to in subdivision 2 of this opinion, changes which have taken place since 1838—constitute, in the opinion of the court, an answer to this question. The most marked justice of which this distribution is susceptible will be attained by carrying it back to the time of the treaty and doing now as would have been done then, treating every individual Indian as every other individual Indian is treated. If these Indian communities had continued to exist as they once existed, each community occupying its own territory and every daughter of every tribe, and they only remaining always the only daughters and the only mothers of the tribe, it would have been feasible to distribute the fund accordingly, disregarding the minor changes made by prosperity or adversity and natural growth or natural decay. But in the existing condition of affairs, it seems wisest and most just to make the first basis of distribution the final basis of distribution, to distribute the fund as the land would have been distributed in 1838—equally to each and all.

A decree will be entered in this case following the form of that which was entered in the case of Whitmire, trustee v. the Cherokee Nation (30 C. Cls. R. 490) and in accordance with the directions heretofore set forth in this opinion. (Petition was filed with the Supreme Court of the United States praying for a writ of mandamus directed to the Court of Claims to compel a modification of the decree entered under the above opinion. The filing of the petition was allowed by the Chief Justice during vacation and an order was issued directed to the Court of Claims to stay the judgment above set out. On consideration of the petition by the full bench of the Supreme Court it was denied and the judgment and decree of the lower court therefore affirmed.)

DEPARTMENT OF THE INTERIOR,
Washington, January 12, 1907.

SIR: Senate bill 7300 which you referred to this Department with request for report thereon for the information of your committee, was sent to the Commissioner of Indian Affairs for examination and report. His report of January 3, 1907, a copy of which is inclosed, gives a very complete history of the matter involved including references to congressional action, the views of the courts, the tribal authorities, and of this Department. The whole matter is so fully presented in this report that it is not deemed necessary to elaborate thereon.

The Department concurs in the conclusion of the Commissioner of Indian Affairs that no change should be made in existing law relating to the enrollment of Choctaw and Chickasaw freedmen and I therefore recommend that the bill do not pass.

The papers are herewith.

Very respectfully,

E. A. HITCHCOCK,
Secretary.

The CHAIRMAN OF THE COMMITTEE ON INDIAN AFFAIRS,
United States Senate.

DEPARTMENT OF THE INTERIOR,
OFFICE OF INDIAN AFFAIRS,
Washington, January 3, 1907

SIR: The office is in receipt of Department letter of December 19, 1906, transmitting for immediate report a communication from the chairman of the Senate Committee on Indian Affairs, dated December 18 1906, inclosing S 7300 being "A bill to amend an act entitled 'An act to provide for the final disposition of the affairs of the Five Civilized Tribes in the Indian Territory and for other purposes,' approved April 26, 1906 "

The bill is as follows

' *Be it enacted by the Senate and House of Representatives of the United States of America in Congress assembled* That section four of an act entitled An act to provide for the final disposition of the affairs of the Five Civilized Tribes in the Indian Territory, and for other purposes,' approved April twenty-sixth, nineteen hundred and six be, and the same is hereby, amended by adding the following proviso at the end of the section

"*And provided further*, That the Secretary of the Interior is hereby authorized and directed to transfer from the Choctaw and Chickasaw freedmen rolls to the rolls of citizens by blood of said nations the name of any person who is of Indian blood or descent on either his or her mother's or father's side, as shown by either the tribal rolls, the records prepared by and in the custody of the Commission to the Five Civilized Tribes or the Department of the Interior or by any governmental records in the possession of any bureau division, or commission of any of the Departments of the Government or any of the courts of Indian Territory *Provided, however*, That nothing herein shall be construed so as to permit the filing of any original application for the enrollment of any person not heretofore, and at the time of the passage of this act, enrolled as a freedman of either the Choctaw or Chickasaw nations or who has an undetermined application for such enrollment now pending, it being the purpose of this act to provide only for a correction of the enrollment of persons of Choctaw or Chickasaw Indian blood who have been enrolled as freedmen of said nations, and no limitation of time within which to file original applications, or to perfect appeals, heretofore fixed by law shall be construed as a bar to rights conferred by this act "

The purpose of the bill seems to be to change the provisions of existing law, and, as its provisions are mandatory, to take from the Department all discretion in the matter of enrolling persons of Indian and freedman descent and compel their enrollment as citizens by blood of the Choctaw and Chickasaw nations

Section 4 of the act approved April 26 1906 (34 Stat L, 137) provides that no name shall be transferred from the approved freedman or any other roll of the Choctaw or Chickasaw nations to the blood roll "unless the records in charge of the Commissioner to the Five Civilized Tribes shows that application for enrollment as a citizen by blood was made within the time prescribed by law, by or for the party seeking the transfer and said records shall be conclusive evidence as to the fact of such application, unless it is shown by documentary evidence that the Commission to the Five Civilized Tribes actually received such application within the time prescribed by law "

Whatever right the Choctaw and Chickasaw freedmen have to share in the distribution of the land of the Choctaw and Chickasaw nations is derived from the provisions of the treaty of April 28 1866 (14 Stat L, 769), subject to such action as was subsequently taken by the legislative bodies of the respective tribes and by Congress

Article 3 of said treaty provides in part that

"The Choctaws and Chickasaws, in consideration of the sum of three hundred thousand dollars, hereby cede to the United States the territory west of the 98° west longitude known as the leased district, provided that the said sum shall be invested and held by the United States at an interest not less than five per cent, in trust for the said nations, until the legislatures of the Choctaw and Chickasaw nations, respectively, shall have made such laws, rules and regulations as may be necessary to give all persons of African descent, resident in the said nations at the date of the treaty of Fort Smith, and their descendants, heretofore held in slavery among said nations, all the rights, privileges, and immunities, including the right of suffrage, of citizens of said nations except in the annuities moneys, and public domain claimed by, or belonging to, said nations, respectively, and also to give to such persons who were residents as aforesaid and their descendants, forty acres each of the land of said nations on the same terms as the Choctaws and Chickasaws to be selected on the survey of said land, after the Choctaws and Chickasaws, and Kansas Indians have made their selections as herein provided "

The act of Congress approved May 17 1882 (22 Stat L, 68, 73), provides, among other things

"That either of said tribes (Choctaw or Chickasaw) may, before such expenditure, adopt and provide for the freedmen in said tribe in accordance with said third article and in such case the money herein provided for such education in said tribe shall be paid over to said tribe, to be taken from the unpaid balance of the three hundred thousand dollars due said tribe."

Pursuant to the provisions of said act, the national council of the Choctaw Nation passed an act as follows, which was approved by the principal chief on May 21, 1883:

"SEC. 1. *Be it enacted by the general council of the Choctaw Nation assembled,* That all persons of African descent resident in the Choctaw Nation at the date of the treaty of Fort Smith, Sept. 13, 1865, and their descendants, formerly held in slavery by the Choctaws or Chickasaws, are hereby declared to be entitled to and invested with all the rights, privileges, and immunities, including the right of suffrage, of citizens of the Choctaw Nation, except in the annuities, moneys, and the public domain of the nation.

"SEC. 2. *Be it further enacted,* That all said persons of African descent as aforesaid, and their descendants, shall be allowed the same rights of process, civil and criminal, in the several courts of this nation as are allowed to Choctaws; and free protection of person and property is hereby granted to all such persons.

"SEC. 3. *Be it further enacted,* That all said persons are hereby declared to be entitled to forty acres each of the lands of the nation, to be selected and held by them under the same title and upon the same terms as the Choctaws.

"SEC. 4. *Be it further enacted,* That all said persons aforesaid are hereby declared to be entitled to equal educational privileges and facilities with the Choctaws, so far as neighborhood schools are concerned.

"SEC. 5. *Be it further enacted,* That all said persons as shall elect to remove and do actually and permanently remove from the nation are hereby declared to be entitled to one hundred dollars per capita, as provided in said 3rd article of the treaty of 1866.

"SEC. 6. *Be it further enacted,* That all said persons who shall decline to become citizens of the Choctaw Nation and who do not elect to remove permanently from the nation are hereby declared to be intruders on the same footing as other citizens of the United States resident herein, and subject to removal for similar causes.

"SEC. 7. *Be it further enacted,* That intermarriage with such freedmen of African descent who were formerly held as slaves of the Choctaws and have become citizens, shall not confer any rights of citizenship in this nation; and all freedmen who have married or who may hereafter marry freedwomen, who have become citizens of the Choctaw Nation, are subject to the permit laws and allowed to remain during good behavior only.

"SEC. 8. *Be it further enacted,* That all such persons of African descent who have become citizens of the Choctaw Nation shall be entitled to hold any office of trust or profit in this nation, except the office of principal chief, and district chiefs.

"SEC. 9. *Be it further enacted,* That the national secretary shall furnish a certified copy of this to the Secretary of the Interior.

"And this act shall take effect and be in force from and after its passage."

On October 26, 1883, the principal chief of the Choctaw Nation approved an act of the council of that nation repealing section 8 of the act of May 21, 1883. Subsequently a question arose as to whether the act of the national council of the Choctaw Nation adopting the freedmen was sufficient for the purpose intended. The Secretary of the Interior, under date of February 26, 1884, said:

"I am of the opinion that the statute now under consideration, as amended by the subsequent law referred to, is a reasonable, substantial, and sufficient compliance with the provision made therefor in the act of May 17, 1882 (22 Stat. L., 73), and of the third article of the treaty therein referred to."

An act of the national council of the Choctaw Nation, approved by the principal chief on October 30, 1888, is as follows:

"1. *Be it enacted by the general council of the Choctaw Nation assembled:* It shall not be lawful for a Choctaw and a negro to marry; and if a Choctaw man or Choctaw woman should marry a negro man or negro woman, he or she shall be deemed guilty of a felony, and shall be proceeded against in the circuit court of the Choctaw Nation having jurisdiction, the same as all other felonies are proceeded against; and if proven guilty shall receive fifty lashes on the bare back." (See Choctaw Laws, 1894 edition, page 206.)

The foregoing, I believe, conclusively shows that it was never the intention of the Choctaw and Chickasaw Indians or the Government that persons who descended from former slaves of Choctaw or Chickasaw Indians, even though such persons are in part of Choctaw or Chickasaw Indian blood, should be allowed to share in the Choctaw and Chickasaw property in excess of an allotment of 40 acres each.

However, with reference to the enrollment of freedmen in these nations, I have the honor to invite your attention to the acts of June 28, 1898 (30 Stat. L., 495), and July 1, 1902 (32 Stat. L., 641). Section 21 of the act of June 28, 1898, provides that the Commission to the Five Civilized Tribes "shall make a correct roll of all Choctaw freedmen entitled to citizenship under the treaties and laws of the Choctaw Nation, and all their descendants born to them since the date of the treaty," and declares that a correct roll shall be made of the Chickasaw freedmen entitled to "rights or benefits" under the treaty of 1866 " and their descendants born to them since the date of said treaty " and that forty acres of land, including their present residences and improvements shall be allotted to each to be selected, held, and used by them until their rights under said treaty shall be determined in such manner as shall be hereafter provided by Congress "

Section 29 of this act says " That the said Choctaw and Chickasaw freedmen who may be entitled to allotments of forty acres each shall be entitled each to land equal in value to forty acres of the average land of the two nations "

No change in the manner of enrolling and making allotments to Choctaw and Chickasaw freedmen was made by the act of July 1, 1902, but section 36 thereof authorized suit to be brought in the Court of Claims for the purpose of determining the right of the Chickasaw freedmen to share in the distribution of the lands of the Choctaw and Chickasaw nations

An appeal to the Supreme Court was provided for and it was declared that allotments should be made to " Chickasaw freedmen and their descendants as provided in the Atoka agreement " (act of June 28, 1898) and that if the courts found that the Chickasaw freedmen were not entitled to allotments independently of the act of July 1, 1902 the appraised value of the land, for the purpose of allotment " allotted to the Chickasaw freedmen should be ascertained and paid to the nations by the United States

As hereinbefore said, the proposed legislation is directory and if enacted will require that any person of freedman and Indian descent who has been enrolled as a freedman or has an application for such enrollment pending at the time of the approval of the act shall be enrolled as a citizen by blood This measure seems to be based on the conclusions reached in the Joe and Dillard Perry case On November 26, 1904, this office expressed the opinion that under the Department s holding of July 11, 1903, in the John W. Shirley case who was an applicant for enrollment as a citizen by blood of the Cherokee Nation Joe and Dillard Perry were entitled to have their names transferred from the freedmen to the blood roll of the Chickasaw Nation Joe and Dillard Perry are the children of Eliza and Charley Perry Eliza Perry it seems is one-fourth Indian one-fourth white and one-half negro or one-half white and one-half negro-Chickasaw freedman Her exact descent can not be determined from the record in the case The father Charley Perry is a recognized citizen by blood of the Chickasaw Nation and the record in the case does not show whether his Chickasaw blood is mixed Eliza and Charley Perry cohabitated as husband and wife and Joe was born on March 20, 1892 Dillard was born on May 5, 1894

On February 21, 1905 the Assistant Attorney-General after discussing the case at length said

I am, therefore clearly of the opinion that applicants are entitled to be transferred to the of roll of Chickasaws by blood '

In opinion of November 11, 1905 he said

' I therefore am advised of no objection to the marriage of these parties except the admission of the mother that about two years before meeting with Perry and about four years prior to her marriage to him she was married to James who may have then been living, though that fact is left in doubt Upon such facts I was February 21 1905 of opinion that Joe and Dillard Perry were shown to be descendants of Charley Perry a recognized citizen of the Chickasaw Nation born within the nation and to its allegiance '

And further

' In the Chickasaw Nation freedmen are not citizens but are a class of noncitizen persons resident within the Chickasaw Nation to whom certain rights are granted by the nation and the Congress of the United States Were they a class of citizens then application would not be within the meaning of the limitation in the act of 1902, supra, one for enrollment but for correction of the record by their removal from one class of citizens to another class of citizens Freedmen not being citizens of the Chickasaw Nation the application can not be considered as one to correct the record but to admit and enroll them into a citizenship to which they previously did not belong and their right to which the record shows had not been asserted or applied for Then application was therefore within the limitation of section 31 of the act of 1902, supra and was made too late

*   *   *   *   *   *   *

"The applicants are enrolled freedmen and having selected allotments as such, were entitled to hold them until their right to enrollment as citizens was fully established, and their allotments if canceled should be reinstated "

It will be observed that in this opinion it was held that these applicants were not entitled to have their names transferred from the freedmen to the blood roll solely because it was not shown at that time that application for their enrollment as citizens by blood was made within the time prescribed by law

It was subsequently shown that the mother of these applicants made application for their enrollment as citizens by blood in 1896 in accordance with the provisions of the act of June 10 1896 (29 Stat L 339) and that their application had been 'impliedly denied On July 17 1906 the Office transmitted the record relative to the application of Joe and Dillard Perry for a transfer of their names from the freedmen to the blood roll of the Chickasaw Nation, and as it was shown that application for their enrollment was made by their mother in 1896 under the act of June 10 1896 (29 Stat L 339, said that under the opinions of the Assistant Attorney-General of February 21 and November 11 1905 the applicants were entitled to enrollment as citizens by blood, and on September 26 1906 the Assistant Attorney-General held that they were not barred by the former adverse decision of the Commission and are entitled to be enrolled as citizens of the nation to the allegiance to which they were born '

The Supreme Court of the United States in the case of The United States v The Choctaw Nation and the Chickasaw Nation (193 U S 115) held that the Chickasaw freedmen were not citizens of that nation and that whatever right they have to share in the distribution of the land of the Choctaw and Chickasaw nations is by virtue of the provisions of the act of July 1 1902 (31 Stat L 641), and not independently thereof '

The foregoing has been brought to your attention at length in order that the facts as to what has been done by Congress the courts and the tribal authorities and what has been said by the Department and the Office on the subject may be clearly before you and Congress should a copy of the report be forwarded to that body I shall now discuss the bill in a general way

As I have already said whatever rights the freedmen have either Choctaw or Chickasaw are based on the provisions of the treaty of 1866 and such subsequent action as was taken by Congress and the tribal authorities and it has always been the understanding of this Office that a person who descended from a freedwoman was recognized by the tribal authorities as a freedman irrespective of the quantum of Indian blood he had

In the days of slavery a child followed the status of the mother, that is a child born of a free mother was free but one born of a slave mother was a slave, and while it is probable that the tribal custom is understood by this Office, grew out of slavery, it is the universal custom among white people of the United States to recognize as a negro any person who is known to be in part of negro blood no matter how small the degree of such blood may be But in order to be absolutely certain as to the prevailing custom in the Choctaw and Chickasaw nations the Office on December 26 1906, wired the Commissioner to the Five Civilized Tribes as follows

' Is it a fact that the tribal authorities of the Choctaw and Chickasaw nations in enrolling persons of freedman and Indian descent enrolled them as freedmen, irrespective of whether the freedman descent was on the side of the father or mother or did they hold that children followed the status of the mother' Rush '

To which the Acting Commissioner replied under date of December 27 1906 saying

"Replying your telegram 26th instant tribal authorities of Choctaw and Chickasaw nations in preparing tribal rolls enrolled children of Indian women by freedmen fathers as Indians Tribal rolls clearly indicate that children of mixed freedmen and Indian descent followed status of mother

I especially invite your attention to the fact that Congress, by section 21 of the act of June 28 1898 in directing the enrollment of Choctaw freedmen used the words And all their descendants born to them since the date of the treaty ' and with reference to the enrollment of Chickasaw freedmen said And their descendants born to them since the date of said treaty '

While the words used authorizing the enrollment of Choctaw freedmen differ slightly from those directing the enrollment of Chickasaw freedmen the meaning is the same, and it seems to have been the intention of Congress to declare that any person who descended from a Choctaw or Chickasaw freedman should be enrolled as a freedman and allowed to share in the distribution of the funds of the nations as such

Ten thousand one hundred and ninety-six persons have been enrolled as Choctaw or Chickasaw freedmen some applications are still pending, and if any of them have been unjustly enrolled as freedmen, the law as it now stands clothes the Department with power sufficient to transfer their names from the freedmen to the blood roll and to enroll as Indians by blood those whose applications have not been passed on if application for enrollment by blood was made within the required time so I do not believe that it would be wise at this late date, or just to the Choctaw and Chickasaw nations, for Congress to reopen the whole matter of the enrollment of Choctaw and Chickasaw freedmen, and declare that the Department arbitrarily enroll as an Indian by blood any person who is of Indian and freedman blood.

The Choctaw and Chickasaw nations have been far more generous to their former slaves and their descendants than the white people have to their ex-slaves. They have allowed them an interest in their lands, which the white slave owners did not do, and have permitted them to use the lands of the nations for more than forty years without paying one cent of rent therefor, and it seems to me that when the custom of the tribes is considered, and the declaration of Congress with reference to their enrollment given the weight to which it is entitled, and the fact recalled that the Choctaw freedman had no rights in the lands of the nations until May 21, 1883, and the Chickasaw freedmen not until July 1, 1902, any fair mind can only conclude that no change should be made in existing law relating to the enrollment of Choctaw and Chickasaw freedmen, and that the recognized custom of the Choctaws and Chickasaws, in force for years, should be followed in making the Choctaw and Chickasaw freedman rolls.

I have the honor to recommend, therefore, that you advise the chairman of the Senate Committee on Indian Affairs that in the opinion of the Department substantial justice will be done the Choctaw and Chickasaw freedmen in the matter of their enrollment under the law as it now stands, and that the bill should not pass.

Very respectfully,

F. E. LEUPP, *Commissioner.*

The SECRETARY OF THE INTERIOR.

O

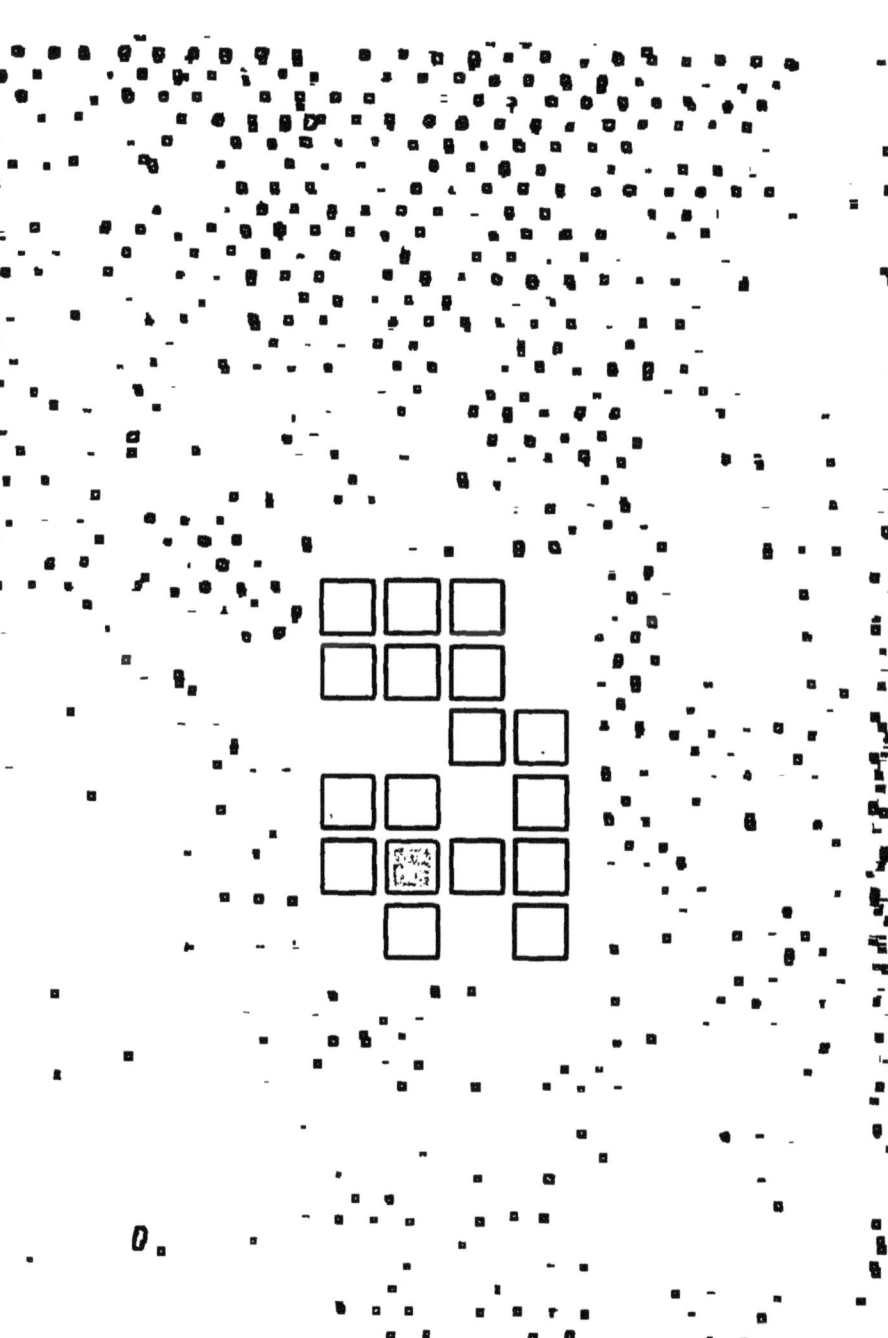

Lightning Source UK Ltd.
Milton Keynes UK
UKHW021837110321
380204UK00003B/270